MICHIGAN REMEMBERED

MICHIGAN REMEMBERED

PHOTOGRAPHS FROM THE FARM SECURITY ADMINISTRATION AND THE OFFICE OF WAR INFORMATION, 1936–1943

Edited by Constance B. Schulz
with Introductory Essays by Constance B. Schulz and William H. Mulligan, Jr.

WAYNE STATE UNIVERSITY PRESS
DETROIT

Great Lakes Books
A complete listing of the books in this series can be found at the back of this volume.

Philip P. Mason, Editor
Department of History, Wayne State University

Dr. Charles K. Hyde, Associate Editor
Department of History, Wayne State University

Library of Congress Cataloging-in-Publication Data

Michigan remembered : photographs from the Farm Security Administration and the Office of War Information, 1936-1943 / edited by Constance B. Schulz ; with introductory essays by Constance B. Schulz and William H. Mulligan, Jr.
    p. cm. — (Great Lakes books)
  ISBN 0-8143-2820-2 (cloth : alk. paper)
   1. Michigan—Social life and customs—20th century—Pictorial works.
   2. Michigan—Pictorial works. 3. Depressions—1929—Michigan—Pictorial works. I. Schulz, Constance B. II. United States. Farm Security Administration. III. United States. Office of War Information. IV. Title. V. Series.
    F567 .M57 2001
    977.4′043—dc21
                            00-011799

Frontispiece photo: Aug. 1942, Detroit. Cadillac Square. John Vachon. USW3-7077-D
Book designed by Mary Claire Krzewinski

FOR CARL,
WHO LOVED MICHIGAN
ALL OF HIS LIFE

CONTENTS

PREFACE

This book is not a photographic album. *Webster's New Collegiate Dictionary* (1976) defines an *album* as "a book with blank pages used for making a collection (as of autographs, stamps, or photographs)." These photographs were not "collected" from a variety of different sources; rather, they have been carefully selected from a single source, the files of the "Historical Section" of the Farm Security Administration (FSA) and the Office of War Information (OWI), whose nearly 110,000 photographs were created (77,000) or gathered (30,000) by that agency as the central work it was authorized to do during the years 1935–43. When the "Historical Section" was disbanded in 1943, its photographic files were given to the Library of Congress, where they now reside.

Instead of an album, this is a collection of historical documents, in which the documents presented for the reader to study and enjoy are photographic rather than textual. Photographs, like any set of documents, on one level seem to speak directly to us about the events or the people they represent and describe. They have an immediacy that reaches across time without any apparent need for the intervention of interpreters or explanation. On another level, photographs, like all documents, are a product of particular circumstances and particular vantage points, were created for a particular purpose, and exist in their particular form as a result of specific choices made by the photographer, the subject, or even the one who directed that the document/photograph be made. The more we know about what was going on when they were made, who created them and why, how the images in them were selected or framed, and what purpose they were meant to serve, the better we will understand them and the more clearly they will speak to us.

These photographs of Michigan, then, are meant on the one hand to be appreciated for themselves. It is hoped that each person who sees them will find something in them that will serve as an aid to remembrance of things past, of particular places familiar to those who call Michigan home, or as an introduction for those who come to it from elsewhere and want to better understand its current landscapes and people by seeing for themselves what once was. We invite readers to look directly at the photographs for the memories they invoke, with the pleasure of recognition or of discovery, and to enjoy their fine photographic quality. At the same time, however, these photographs are evidence about the past that need a context and an explanation to make their rich layers of meaning come alive. We hope that those who have enjoyed the images for their nostalgic evocations and visual richness will also turn to the texts that accompany them, which seek to provide a context for them. This is done in three ways:

- The introductory essay by William H. Mulligan, Jr., is a brief overview of the momentous events that occurred in or had a direct impact on Michigan in the tumultuous decades of the 1930s and the 1940s, because for many who now live in Michigan the events of fifty-five to sixty years ago are dimly, if at all, remembered or understood.

- My introductory essay tells the story of the federal agency of whose records these photographs are a part, because the nature of that agency had an important impact on the photographic images its photographers created. In particular, this section examines the importance to the agency and its mission of Roy Stryker, the man who headed it throughout its existence. In addition, it includes brief biographies of the six men who photographed events in Michigan for the files of the FSA/OWI.

- The roughly chronological groups of photographs represent geographic and economic regions within Michigan, because the photographs themselves were taken in particular places. Each group of photographs has a brief introduction that sets the scene by describing which photographers took them, what their assignment was, and something about the region or the time they were photographing. More description or background is provided where appropriate.

A summary of the method by which the photographs were chosen, and an explanation of the captions that appear with each image, is in order. The more than 2,500 images of Michigan in the Library of Congress "Farm Security Administration and Office of War Information Collection" exist in two different physical forms. The microfilm version of the FSA/OWI file contains eighty-one "lots," or groups, of photographs of Michigan, each of which includes the photos taken by one or two photographers working in a specific place at a particular time. Lot 810, for instance, contains 170 photographs by Arthur Siegel of the drug manufacturing operations at Parke-Davis & Co. in Detroit in May 1943. A graduate student at the University of South Carolina worked from the microfilm to create a complete database of all caption information (including place, date, and name of the photographer) for the photographs in the Michigan "lots." From this preliminary study of the images as they appear in the microfilm, I selected and made a "reader-printer" paper copy of nearly five hundred photographs.

The Michigan photographs also exist as file prints made between 1935 and 1943 by the FSA/OWI laboratory staff. Pasted on cardboard mounts and identified with a caption and a negative number, these are now kept in reference file cabinets in the Prints and Photographs (P&P) Division reading room in the Madison Building of the Library of Congress. There they are kept in the order in which they were rearranged in a complicated geographic and topical system shortly before their donation to the Library. Michigan is one of six states from the Great Lakes region from which photographs were interfiled under such broad topics as "The Land," "Cities and Towns," "People as Such," "Work," and so on. I went through all of the file drawers in the P&P reading room in which Michigan photographs appeared, checking the photographic quality of those selected from microfilm in the preliminary process against the actual photographs, sometimes choosing new images. In both parts of the process, I chose photographs partly on the basis of their aesthetic appeal and photographic quality, but also with the aim of representing as much as possible the range of topics and geographic regions of the state present in the file, and telling a cohesive story.

The captions that appear in this book are the captions originally given each image by the photographers themselves in consultation with Roy Stryker and later edited by Paul Vanderbilt and his staff. The introduction briefly describes how that process worked at the agency. Although the captions are usually short, sometimes repetitive, and occasionally use terms not current today (for example, "Negro" instead of "African American"), they have been included virtually unchanged as an essential piece of evidence about the era in which the photographs were taken and distributed. The only changes made have been silent corrections of typographical errors in the spelling, and a shift of the order in which the place, date, and photographer's name appear. The negative numbers given for each photograph are those for the remastered negatives (duplicated from the original FSA/OWI negatives) created by the Library of Congress in a recent conservation project. Anyone wishing a copy of a particular image can use that number to order it directly from the Library's Photoduplication Service.

In 1992, the Library of Congress began to make the whole of its FSA/OWI collection available in an electronic form, through the Prints and Photographs Online Catalog. To locate images reproduced in this book through that catalog, simply type in the negative number appearing under each photograph, preceded by the lettters "LC," when prompted for a search term. Those who have enjoyed looking at the images in this book can find more examples of fine photography in the library's collections, available from the Division's homepage:

http://lcweb.loc.gov/rr/print

I have enjoyed the help of a number of individuals and institutions, who have made this book possible. Two graduate students in the Applied History Program at the University of South Carolina have performed crucial tasks: Daniel Vivian patiently scrolled through all of the images on microfilm to create the database of caption information, from which Laura Benson created the final caption list of the selected photographs. In addition, Elisa Schulz not only provided me with a place to stay near the Library of Congress for the many days of research needed to select images and track down information about photographers, she also performed the invaluable task of proofreading lists of negative numbers and caption information.

The scholarly community of those who study the FSA/OWI photographic corpus are indebted to the custodians of the rich body of primary sources that make that study possible, and I owe a special debt of gratitude to the staff of the Prints and Photographs Division of the Library of Congress. Although all the staff there are unfailingly helpful, particular thanks must go to Beverly W. Brannan, Barbara Natanson, and Megan Keister. James C. "Andy" Anderson at the University of Louisville's Photographic Archives, Barb Krieger at the Dartmouth College Archives, and the reference staff at the art reference library and the Archives of American Art of the Smithsonian Institution all provided cheerful assistance in answer to particular and general questions about the Michigan FSA photographers and their work.

Constance B. Schulz

INTRODUCTION

Michigan in the Great Depression: The Dream Lost, the Dream Reclaimed

William H. Mulligan, Jr.
Department of History
Murray State University

The first three decades of the twentieth century saw the transformation of the American economy in ways that changed the lives of nearly all Americans. The old economy, based on the construction of canals, railroads, and other large-scale infrastructure projects, gave way with increasing speed after the First World War to an economy based on the manufacture of consumer products and on consumer spending. The new economy featured a vast array of new products based on and manufactured with new technologies. This new economy seemed ready to reward working Americans for their generations of hard work and to provide them with a level of comfort and security of which they had previously only dreamed.[1]

This new national economy brought great change to Michigan and moved the state to the center of the national economy and the national consciousness. The focus of the new economy was on the mass production of a wide variety of consumer products, and no consumer product more visibly or dramatically changed the nation than the automobile. No place was more involved with producing automobiles than Michigan. This made Detroit, now internationally known as the Motor City, the epicenter for the changes rippling through the nation. Henry Ford put a human face and personality on the new, affordable car and the industry that produced it. His Model T became an integral part not only of the national economy, but also of the national culture of the 1920s.

Detroit and the other cities that manufactured automobiles, especially Dearborn and Flint, grew rapidly. The demand for city services and basic amenities, such as housing, in these areas was so great that they strained to keep up with it, and often fell far behind.[2] Immigrants from southern and eastern Europe, Mexico, and the Middle East flocked to the opportunities the expanding automobile and other new industries offered, as did residents of Michigan's rural communities who saw more potential for improving their lives in the factories than on their worn out farms. From as far away as the Copper Country, in the far western end of the Upper Peninsula, where the mines had never recovered from the collapse of the copper market at the end of the First World War, trainloads arrived to fill the jobs in the ever-expanding auto plants. These new factories became a source of refuge from the economic dislocation of the postwar period not only for the miners, but also for farmers whose land was exhausted and for immigrants fleeing the chaos and starvation in Europe.

In much of the United States, the rise of manufacturing fueled by unprecedented demand for new consumer products masked weaknesses in agriculture and the other traditional bases of the economy. Nowhere was this more true than in Michigan, the center of the largest of these new industries.

When the new economy faltered and collapsed, the consequences would hit Michigan hard. As late as 1910, more than half of Michigan's population lived in rural areas. By 1920, after two decades of decline in the population of the northern two-thirds of the state, just over 60 percent of Michiganians lived in urban areas, and by 1930 fewer than one in three lived in rural areas. While the country as a whole was moving to the city, the pace was quicker and the change more dramatic in Michigan.

During the 1920s the number of farms in Michigan declined by 13.5 percent (compared with a national decline of only 2.3 percent) and farm acreage in the state declined by 10.5 percent. Farms in Michigan were being abandoned, not consolidated. Farm prices had fallen from the high levels reached during the First World War, leaving farmers unable to pay their mortgages and other debts. By 1928, nine million acres in Michigan were tax delinquent—and the crash was yet to come.

Farming areas in Michigan were not alone in losing population. Houghton County, center of the state's copper mining industry, lost 20,000 in population during the 1920s, and fully half of its 1910 population by 1940. The other copper and iron mining areas in the Upper Peninsula also lost substantial portions of their populations during this period.

Michigan as a whole grew rapidly, however, increasing in population from 3.668 million to 4.842 million between 1920 and 1930, its second consecutive decade of more than 30 percent growth. This growth was highly concentrated in the southern third of the state, especially in the industrial cities of Detroit, Pontiac, Flint, Saginaw, Jackson, Lansing, Grand Rapids, and Muskegon. With this growth came a change in the character of the state's population, significantly increasing the proportion of Catholics and Jews as well as bringing many native white fundamentalist Protestants and African Americans from the American South.

By the end of the 1920s Michigan was a far different place than it had been only a few decades earlier. No longer on the fringes of the national economy, Michigan had been propelled by the automobile into a leading role in the booming economy of the 1920s.

In 1928, despite all of these changes, Michigan continued its long tradition of support for the Republican Party and voted for Herbert Hoover in the presidential election. His promise that poverty would soon be eliminated seemed almost cautious after the tremendous economic progress so many had enjoyed in the decades just past. Surely poverty and need were about to disappear forever.

When the stock market collapsed in October 1929, its effect on the people of Michigan was not clear at first. It must certainly have seemed unlikely to the state's factory workers, miners, and farmers that they would be affected at all by the problems of something as far away and as abstract as the stock market. Yet, with ever increasing momentum, Michigan's new industrial economy slowed, putting people out of work. Auto production fell from more than 5 million units in 1929 to only 1.3 million in 1932. Iron production plummeted from an average of 15 million tons during the 1920s to only 1 million in 1932.[3] Employment in the mines declined from 9,000 in 1929 to 2,700 in 1933. In Dickinson County on the Menominee Range only one of forty mines was in operation in 1935.[4] Farmers, miners, factory workers—everyone in the state—soon faced the harsh reality of fewer hours, less pay, and for many no work at all.

The new industrial cities had been straining to deal with the rapid growth that prosperity had brought; now they faced the challenge of massive under- and unemployment. Those who had left their homes in Europe, Mexico, and the Middle East, the South, and rural Michigan faced the crisis without the support of extended families and kin. Survival now became their greatest challenge.

Unemployment settled quickly over industrial Michigan. By March 1930 the situation was so desperate that there were demonstrations by unemployed industrial workers in Detroit, Grand Rapids, Flint, Muskegon, and Kalamazoo. The Detroit demonstration was broken up by mounted policemen; dozens were injured and more than thirty arrested.

Detroit, the center of the new industrial economy, became the focal point for dealing with the problems of massive industrial unemployment. As early as December 1929 outgoing Mayor John Lodge appointed a Mayor's Labor Committee to study unemployment. He was succeeded as mayor early in the new year by Charles Bowles. When Bowles was unable to deal effectively with the problems unemployment created in the city, and city police used night sticks to disperse a protest by unemployed workers in March, he was recalled and replaced by Recorder's Court judge Frank Murphy.

Murphy promised a "new deal" in city government and argued that government had a legitimate role to play as champion of the underprivileged. He outlined a new approach to governmental responsibility for those in need. Relief, according to Murphy, was "the duty of the state . . . not a matter of charity, and . . . not paternally, but as a matter of right."[5] The mayor of a city, he said, "must have ears sensitive to the pleadings and protests of all who hunger for the social justice the day demands."[6] Murphy backed up his words with action. Immediately after the election he appointed a Mayor's Committee against Unemployment and began an aggressive attack on the problem of unemployment in Detroit. The scope of the problem, it soon became clear, was staggering and unprecedented. By late 1930 city relief efforts were costing $2 million a month and assisting 46,000 families. Twelve percent of Detroiters were on relief.

When a second rally of the unemployed was held to demand direct relief in October of 1931, Murphy did not have city police disperse the crowd, as Bowles had done, but spent several hours meeting with a committee of demonstrators. Murphy was elected to a full two-year term in 1931 and brought tremendous energy and commitment to the office of mayor. The city's and state's economic situation continued, however, to decline.

Unlike many major cities which had traditionally relied on private organizations to help those in need, Detroit had a long tradition of public relief. Even before Murphy began his relief efforts, fully 97.7 percent of relief in Detroit was provided by the city government, compared with 56.4 percent on average in seventy-four other large cities. A number of private agencies in Detroit did supplement city efforts to help meet the needs of those who had been thrown out of work. Their efforts were dwarfed by the size of the problem, and the large number of appeals met with increasingly small returns. When United States Senator James Couzens offered to provide $1 million of his own money for relief if the city could raise $9 million to match it, only $651,000 could be raised.

The scale of the unemployment and relief problems in Detroit was daunting, by November 1932 about 50 percent of wage earners in the city were out of work. The Mayor's Unemployment Committee had registered more than 118,000 unemployed men and women by July 1, 1931. At the massive Ford Rouge Plant in Dearborn, in many ways the symbol of the new industrial economy, employment fell from 98,337 in 1929 to 28,915 by 1933.[7]

Under Murphy's leadership the Department of Public Welfare provided grocery vouchers and helped with rent, utilities, and insurance premium payments. Medical care was provided at the city's Receiving Hospital or in private hospitals and clinics. The city established a free employment bureau to help people find jobs. While the bureau was able to locate 25,000 jobs, there were still some 200,000 out of work. The Homeless Men's Bureau helped provide lodging and meals, initially using the idle Fisher Body Division plant at West Ford and 23rd and Studebaker's Plant 10. Homeless women were cared for by a variety of religious and secular organizations. Warehouses throughout the city were opened as shelters for the homeless.

While Republican governor Wilber M. Brucker stuck with the Hoover plan of limited government intervention in the economy, Murphy and other local leaders in Detroit and across the state were forced to deal with the human cost of the economic collapse. The relief burden was too great, however, for the city to carry alone for long. Despite Murphy's pledge that no one in Detroit would be allowed to go hungry or be cold, go without housing, or be unclothed, the sheer numbers involved forced an end to cash relief in Detroit in 1931, replaced by food orders, which were reduced from $4 weekly for a husband and wife and an additional $1 per child to a flat $1 a week per person.[8]

Murphy's aggressive program caused severe financial problems for the city as it strained to meet rising relief costs with declining revenue as property taxes went unpaid. Appeals for state assistance led to conflict between Murphy and Governor Brucker, who believed that local communities, not the state, should be responsible for relief. He responded to Murphy's appeals for state aid by blaming the city's financial problems on its overly generous relief program.

When Brucker appointed a State Unemployment Commission in August 1931, it was unfunded. The traditional relief system in the state, supported by the property tax, was overwhelmed by numbers it had never faced before or ever anticipated facing. In Kalkaska County, 85.5 per percent of the population was dependent on relief, according to an April 1932 survey, followed closely by Keweenaw County with 81.5 percent. Lake, Baraga, and Roscommon counties were at 75 percent, and four other counties had more than half their populations on relief. While the proportion in Wayne County was not as large, some 338,000 people were on relief there.[9] With such large-scale unemployment came escalating tax delinquencies, costing all units of government revenue at a time they needed it desperately.

Murphy was emerging as a national leader among mayors who found themselves on the front lines of the effort to deal with the massive human cost of the depression. He called a meeting of Michigan mayors to discuss relief issues in May of 1932 and followed that with a call for a national meeting of mayors of large cities.

In Grand Rapids, hard hit by the decline of its furniture industry, which had begun in 1927, city manager George Welsh developed an imaginative and ambitious response to widespread unemployment and hardship. The city's twelve private welfare agencies were overwhelmed as their caseload grew from its usual level of fewer than two hundred families to thousands as unemployment spread through the furniture city. Welsh agreed to work for $1 per year and took a variety of economy measures, including cutting city salaries by 25 percent. He used the resulting surplus and the city snow removal budget to hire unemployed married men to shovel snow downtown and around city churches and synagogues. When the program was first announced 650 men applied for work. In order to stretch city funds to the maximum, Welsh paid these workers in scrip, redeemable at a city store. The city store offered groceries, shoes and clothing, furniture, and nearly anything else a family needed. While there were complaints from the city's grocers, the AFL-CIO, and the local Carpenters and Joiners Union, Welsh's plan expanded as he identified city projects that could use existing equipment and required little cash. To stretch the city's funds even further, women were hired and paid in scrip to can fruits and vegetables that were sold at the city store.

In July 1931 he entered into an agreement with the state highway department to extend North Division Avenue using 130 unemployed men. Despite Welsh's program, the city welfare budget rose from $3,000 a month early in 1929 to more than $60,000 monthly by the late fall of 1930—approximately one-third of the city budget. By late 1932 Welsh's opponents, who argued that payment in scrip was inefficient and demeaning, forced his resignation and a switch to cash payments. The Grand Rapids work program quickly disappeared, due to the city's lack of cash. During its operation Welsh's program attracted national attention as an innovative and effective way to address the unprecedented levels of unemployment plaguing the nation. Grand Rapids received national publicity as the city where everyone had a job.[10]

The unemployment level in Michigan reached 18 percent in 1931, then rose even higher, to 43 percent in 1932 and 46 percent in 1933. Governor Brucker, however, vetoed legislative measures that would have provided direct relief, unemployment insurance, and aid for the elderly. Instead, he promoted the purchase of Michigan products as a way to restore the economy. Federal efforts, launched reluctantly by President Hoover in 1931, provided $27 million for public works in Michigan, including highways, post offices, and harbor improvements. In 1932, however, of some $30 million spent on relief statewide, $24 million came from cities, townships, and counties.

In 1932, Democrat William A. Comstock defeated Brucker for governor and the Democratic Party gained control of both houses of the state legislature. Comstock had lost the 1926, 1928, and 1930 gubernatorial elections by sizable margins—in 1928 by more than two to one to Fred Green and in 1930 to Brucker by more than 125,000 of some 850,000 votes cast. Further, between 1921 and 1925 there had not been a single Democrat in either house of the legislature. Comstock's victory marked a significant political change for Michigan. In 1932 more than 1.6 million Michiganians voted—a remarkable increase of nearly 100 percent, due, no doubt, to the nation's deepening economic crisis and the vigorous Roosevelt presidential campaign—and charted a very different political course for the state.

Comstock found the state in dire straits. Unemployment was continuing to rise—it would hit nearly 50 percent statewide in 1933. Delinquencies on property taxes, the basic source of revenue for every level of government in Michigan, far exceeded those in every other state. This was due not only to the economic crisis, but also to the nearly 500 percent increase in property taxes that had occurred in the state between 1914 and 1930. Comstock was not a radical reformer or even a New Dealer. He had argued during the campaign that direct relief would undermine public morale. He faced a greater crisis than unemployment when he took office, however.

Roughly one in four of the state's banks, more than two hundred, had already failed since the onset of the economic crisis, and there were strong rumors that Detroit's two largest bank holding companies would soon follow. The Guardian Detroit Union Group and the Detroit Bankers Company controlled banks not only in Detroit and its suburbs, but throughout the state as well. The undertow from their collapse would devastate the state. One of Governor Comstock's first actions was to declare a state bank holiday from February 14–23, which was followed by a federal bank holiday after Roosevelt's inauguration on March 4. The banking crisis led to the merger of the two holding companies as the new National Bank of Detroit, and depositors faced serious restrictions on how much money they could withdraw. The entire city endured a cash crunch for several months. In Grand Rapids only three of eight banks reopened after the bank holiday.

Both the Unemployed Citizens' League of Michigan and the Michigan Labor and Commodities Exchange tried to establish barter systems to help people deal with the cash shortage caused by the prolonged bank holiday. The auto companies were able to draw on cash deposited outside the state, but smaller firms faced serious challenges meeting their payrolls and paying their bills. The city was able to cash many of its paychecks on February 15, but "passed" on paydays until late April, giving employees food and fuel vouchers instead of cash. The Mayor's Unemployment Commission distributed food baskets to city employees during the crisis, and a City Employees' Relief Committee was formed. The Mayor's Scrip Committee issued nearly $24 million in scrip during the 1933–34 fiscal year which was accepted for taxes and rent. City workers were paid entirely in scrip, and private employers were encouraged to participate. One of the most serious consequences of the state bank holiday was the city's default on its debt when it missed an interest payment the day after the holiday began.

People found ways to deal with the bank closings and the shortage of cash, as Willard J. Prentice recalled:

> I was a cooperative engineering student at the University of Detroit when the government closed the banks. I had only a few dollars in my pocket, which was

soon gone, leaving no money for food. My usual eating place was the Peter Pan Restaurant on Livernois across from the school. The owner was Speros Sassalos, an affable Greek, who had compassion for the students caught in my predicament. I don't know how many took advantage of his generosity, but "Doc" Speros, as he was known to the students, fed us "on the cuff." My parents lived in Douglas, Allegan County, two hundred miles to the west. Their funds were tied up in the Fruit Growers State Bank of Saugatuck, which, like the Detroit banks, was indefinitely closed. Somehow, after a couple of weeks, my father, Joseph W. Prentice, scraped up a few dollars and bailed me out.[11]

Detroit was not the only governmental unit having financial problems; the demand for government services far exceeded revenues everywhere in Michigan. Every township, city, and county faced unprecedented levels of unemployment and economic hardship. Revenues were steeply reduced by the economic crisis and by previous state policy. A referendum in November 1932 had limited property taxes, and the legislature addressed the problem with a comprehensive reform of state tax policy. In 1933 a sales tax of 3 percent was imposed to fund state government, and all property tax revenues were set aside for local government. Further, the legislature canceled penalties on overdue taxes and postponed tax sales. There had been efforts at intimidation of bidders at farm auctions and demonstrations in both Stanton and Manistee. In 1933 the state began to assess a tax on newly legalized beer, wine, and liquor, and imposed a variety of new taxes to generate revenue over the next several years.

Also in 1933, the state established an old age assistance program which was later revised to conform with the federal social security program when it began in 1937. A Bureau of Social Aid was set up in each county to administer assistance to those over sixty-five. The State Emergency Welfare Relief Commission, set up to coordinate and administer state relief efforts, spent $43 million in its first year, and helped 640,000 people.

The commission found itself with an existing system that assumed those needing help would be few and either lazy or irresponsible. It had to replace the poorhouse, workhouse, or commissary approach—which had sought to make receiving relief public and shameful—with vouchers and soon thereafter checks that allowed people to purchase what they needed. The commission also recognized quickly that people did not just want help; they wanted to work.[12]

With the election in 1932 of Franklin Delano Roosevelt as president, the state began to receive increasing assistance from the federal government. In the summer of 1933 some 640,000 people statewide were receiving assistance, primarily from the state. That year New Deal programs began to provide additional assistance, beginning with the Civil Works Administration (CWA), which employed 170,000. The Works Progress Administration

(WPA), the Civilian Conservation Corps (CCC), and the National Youth Administration (NYA) were especially important relief programs in Michigan. Federal assistance changed the scale of relief efforts exponentially. In Wayne County alone between April 1933 and December 1935, $65 million dollars (80 percent from federal sources) was spent on relief activities. The CCC operated an average of 50 camps a year in Michigan, a total of 103 overall during its existence. The WPA built auditoriums, schools, armories, hospitals, sidewalks, and bridges, among other things, between 1935 and 1942, employing 200,000 at its peak. WPA projects cost $500 million, with three-quarters of that sum coming from the federal government.

In 1934, 12.2 percent of Michigan's families were on some form of relief, but in tiny Keweenaw County in the Upper Peninsula the figure was 66 percent, and it was 33 percent in neighboring Houghton County. Iron-mining counties in the Upper Peninsula were also hard hit, as production plummeted and many mines closed, never to reopen. Recovery in the industry was very slow. Production had reached only eleven million tons in 1939, before the beginning of the Second World War in Europe and U.S. preparation for possible war stimulated demand. There was a small increase in the number of farms in the Upper Peninsula as out-of-work miners and others returned to the land in an attempt to survive.

The surge in relief efforts did not end politics in the state, or even within the Democratic Party. The Democrats divided over the New Deal and its relief and recovery programs. Comstock, who was not an ardent New Dealer, was defeated in the 1934 primary by Arthur J. Lacy, who ran as a strong supporter of the New Deal and President Roosevelt. He was supported by the progressive wing of the state Democratic Party, including Frank Murphy. Lacy, however, was defeated in the general election by Frank Fitzgerald by about 82,000 votes.

During Fitzgerald's administration the New Deal programs continued to form the backbone of relief efforts. A number of agencies offered programs and took on a variety of projects that put people to work.

For example, the CWA constructed a park and golf course in Keweenaw County. Dubbed "Potter's Folly" after Ocha Potter, who had convinced federal relief administrator William Haber to fund the project, construction took place during the winter of 1933–34. By the end of 1934 a nine-hole golf course and a spacious log lodge with two immense stone fireplaces had been completed by 124 workers from Keweenaw County. Potter convinced Haber to add cottages to provide lodging for the golfers, and ten cabins were built by the WPA in late 1935, with ten more added slightly later. Local materials and local craftsmen were used, including Victor Oja, who supervised the construction of the clubhouse, and Louis Azzi, who built the two large stone fireplaces in the lodge.[13]

The WPA also took on the reconstruction of Fort Wilkins in Copper Harbor. Oja again played a leading role, rebuilding every building at the site using lumber cut from the base of nearby Brockway Mountain and local labor to square the large timbers appropriate for the 1840s fort structures. Unemployed miners working on the project blasted through solid rock to create drainage ditches and room for septic tanks.[14]

In addition to these more visible projects, in Houghton County alone some three thousand men were employed building and widening narrow country roads, an activity that took place statewide.[15]

The CWA was replaced in 1935 by the WPA, which built new schools, post offices, and other government buildings. In the four counties of the Copper Country alone, the WPA spent more than $10 million on work projects between 1936 and 1939.[16]

The WPA was not just a construction program; it provided work for individuals in a wide variety of occupations. Historians surveyed county court houses, township halls, and other government buildings for records and published the results of their efforts. Writers assembled guidebooks for every state, playwrights wrote plays, and actors performed them. The WPA also employed musicians, and a variety of federal bands performed across the state. The most visible of the WPA's nonconstruction activities was its program for artists. Often the works were commissioned for buildings built as WPA projects, but not always. The artworks included murals, relief carvings, sculpture, photographs, paintings, prints, posters, art education projects, and at least one publication, *Index of American Design*. Many of the works, like Joe Lasker's mural of copper miners in the Calumet post office, were connected to the history and character of the community in which they were situated. The Frankfort post office mural depicted a shipwreck that had taken place within sight of the building. The Munising post office, located on the shores of Lake Superior, had a mural that presented the Chippewa legend of the creation of the lake's islands. Murals were especially popular, and the artists showed the influence of Diego Rivera's murals in the Detroit Institute of Art and the work of Thomas Hart Benton. The whole program was based on the premise that art could be appreciated by everyone, not just an elite.[17]

While many New Deal programs were explicitly aimed at providing work for male heads of families, NYA provided employment opportunities and job training for young people and worked with colleges to provide jobs for students. One NYA program in the Upper Peninsula taught young men and women wood- and metalworking skills and is, in many ways, typical of how the programs operated. An experienced craftsman, Harold Richards, was hired to teach his skill through a separate federal program, the National Reemployment Service. Shops were set up and equipped in Houghton, Laurium, Calumet, and Mohawk, to be accessible to the students. The workday usually lasted from 8:00 to 4:00, with the students working on a variety of projects, including building file cabinets, desks, toboggans, and other items for military bases. One particular project involved folding chairs. "The chairs had been sent all over the country but no one could get them to lay completely flat when folded. But we worked on it for a couple of months, mostly John [Sibilsky]. He has a genius for that sort of thing. Finally we did it and word came from Washington as special recognition," Richards remembered years later.[18]

The Kent County Airport also benefited greatly from a number of projects funded by several New Deal agencies. Airport administrator Tom Walsh had a plan for its future, but the depression had all but eliminated any chance of funding by the state or county. In 1934 one of the first CWA projects in the nation began implementing his plan by removing an existing hangar and building a new, larger one with a machine shop. The CWA, with additional funding from the Federal Emergency Relief Administration, expanded and paved runways, improved drainage, and installed lighting and a code beacon. The result was an airport with a national reputation for excellence. Walsh continued to develop the airport in partnership with the WPA after 1935. All together, the WPA invested more than $1.5 million in the Kent County Airport.[19]

The CCC provided work for young, unmarried men between the ages of eighteen and twenty-eight. The CCC also hired Local Experienced Men (LEM)to provide experience for the camp work crews as well as work for those who were older than the CCC generally recruited. During its existence the CCC had more than one hundred camps in Michigan and provided jobs for more than one hundred thousand Michiganians.[20] The CCC was especially important in the northern Lower Peninsula and the Upper Peninsula.

Beginning in April 1933, the CCC tackled a variety of fire control projects, working from camps established in cutover and abandoned lands that were especially prone to fire. Camps Raco in the eastern Upper Peninsula; Cusino and Kentucky in Alger County; Steuben near Manistique; and Mack Lake near Mio were among the earliest established. Within six months some sixty-seven miles of fire breaks and more than five hundred miles of truck trails were constructed, along with other fire prevention and fire fighting measures. During the winter of 1933–34, fire towers were built and telephone lines strung connecting them. Forest fire prevention was a major focus of the CCC in Michigan, although they also fought fires, including the major forest fire on Isle Royale in the summer of 1936. The CCC also replanted cutover land and surveyed the boundaries of state forests and game preserves. They built 265 bridges and many buildings.

They were seemingly everywhere in rural Michigan. Base pay was $30 a month, of which $25 was sent home to family, and medical and dental care was provided by military reserve physicians and dentists. Six camps were established for "older men," veterans of the First World War who were outside the program's target age group. The CCC followed contemporary ideas about racial segregation. There was an Indian camp, Camp Marquette, west of Sault Ste. Marie, for Native Americans and there were several camps for African Americans, the first of which was Camp Mack Lake. One of those assigned to Mack Lake was Joseph Louis Barrow—later heavyweight champion of the world as Joe Louis.

The Michigan CCC program planted twice as many trees as in any other state, nearly half a billion, and completed an array of projects. More than $20 million in wages was sent home between April 1933 and the end of the program in June 1942. The CCC camp at Germfask was later used for conscientious objectors, and other Upper Peninsula camps at Pori, Sidnaw, Au Train, Evelyn, and Raco housed German POWs during the Second World War.[21]

Not all of the New Deal programs were for men, although the WPA allowed only one family member to work on its projects, which limited opportunities for women. Women with disabled husbands or elderly parents dependent on them did qualify for office and clerical work. From time to time there were sewing, knitting, quilting, or canning projects for which women were hired. Elizabeth Wahtola took part in one sewing project as an eighteen-year-old girl in Wolverine Location, near Mohawk.

> We had to wear uniforms, blue ones and white caps with the letters "W.P.A."
> Sewing machines were put back in a big room downstairs, where you go through to
> the Police Station. There would be six in a unit, called an 'erg.' Supervisors would
> come and bring bundles. The first woman in the unit would do her step—shirts,
> pants, whatever they had to do. Then it would be passed on to the second one in
> the unit and they'd do their step and so on until everything was completed. Then
> that bundle would be done. Buttonholes would be made by another woman by
> hand. If you made a hundred a day, you were doing good. And they had to be
> perfect, about 18 stitches to an inch. . . . Then it'd be passed on to the pressers
> where they'd be pressed and folded on cardboards like in factories. Pressed real
> neatly just as if you'd bought it.[22]

The federal government had taken over responsibility for relief and reemployment efforts in Michigan with a wide variety of programs. During the early years of this effort, when the focus was clearly on relief, Frank Murphy was out of the country, serving as governor general of the Philippines. This seemed a strange post for Murphy, who had played a leading role among the nation's mayors in dealing with economic crisis and in organizing the National Conference of Mayors, which was a direct consequence of a meeting Murphy had called in Detroit in June 1932. Still, Murphy was in Manila, while his successor in Detroit wrestled with the fiscal and financial aftermath of Murphy's aggressive relief efforts. For all the positive national attention the Murphy programs had attracted as models of government action at the local level, they had left the city with serious financial problems.

In 1936 Murphy returned to Michigan to run for governor against Republican Frank Fitzgerald, who had been elected in 1934, in part, at least, because of a bitter Democratic split over the state tax reforms of 1933 and Governor Comstock's lack of enthusiasm for New Deal programs. Murphy ran on his record as mayor and as an ardent supporter of Roosevelt's New Deal, offering Michigan as a model state to test future New Deal programs. Murphy emphasized his own philosophy of government as an active participant in social reform efforts and as a force for bettering the lives of the less fortunate. While the Democrats decisively gained control of both houses of the legislature, Murphy won by only a narrow margin. Those Democrats who had supported Comstock did not do much to help elect Murphy.

Before he was inaugurated Michigan was again thrust into the nation's spotlight, by the sit-down strike in Flint, and Murphy had to deal with that before he could take up his campaign agenda. The strike had begun in late December 1936 among members of the United Auto Workers (UAW) at Fisher Body Plant Number One and quickly spread throughout Flint.[23] The Flint Strike was the result of long-standing efforts by the UAW to organize General Motors workers and of workers' concerns about job security, working conditions, and wages. General Motors had actively opposed the efforts of the union to organize its workforce and had refused to negotiate or even seriously discuss worker concerns with the union. Once the strike began and workers occupied the plant, General Motors went to court and obtained an injunction ordering the strikers to leave the plant. They refused, and there were scuffles that led to injuries. The potential for more serious violence seemed very real. Murphy called out the National Guard, not to enforce the injunction but to prevent violence while he tried to negotiate a settlement. By February 1937 the strike was over, and a month later an agreement was in place that allowed the UAW to organize all of General Motors. Chrysler quickly also recognized the union, leaving Ford as the only holdout among the major automakers. Murphy emerged as a champion of labor, and his role in ending the strike without violence attracted a great deal of positive attention nationally.

Unionizing Ford proved to be a bloody battle. In May 1937 Walter Reuther and a number of UAW leaders were savagely beaten near the Rouge Plant in Dearborn. Ford conducted an aggressive anti-union intimidation campaign, led by Harry Bennett, but the UAW, protected by the Wagner Act, ultimately prevailed. By mid-1941 Ford had not only recognized the UAW but accepted a closed shop and dues checkoff.

Once the Flint sit-down strike was settled Murphy turned his attention to the agenda he had put forth during his campaign and increased state aid to public schools. He also took up the issues of social security and unemployment insurance as long-term solutions to the problem of economic security for working people, and was one of President Roosevelt's strongest supporters among the nation's governors. His major effort was directed at civil service reform, and he signed a bill creating a state civil service commission to administer a system of hiring state employees on the basis of merit and ending the wholesale turnover of state employees with every election.

In the 1938 election Murphy was defeated by Frank Fitzgerald. None of Murphy's achievements had been without great controversy. His strong support for Roosevelt and the New Deal further alienated the still-potent Comstock wing of the Michigan Democratic Party, as well as many Republicans. His role in the Flint sit-down strike was seen as radically pro-labor by some, but too middle-of-the-road for those on the opposite side of the spectrum. Further, and perhaps more important than any other factor, despite Murphy's best efforts and high ideals about the government's responsibility to help the less fortunate, the economy remained stubbornly inert. The New Deal programs provided income to pay rent and buy food but they did not offer much beyond survival, and they offered little security. The New Deal was keeping people from starving and was maintaining their faith in the capitalist system, but it had not yet brought back prosperity. While Murphy would come to be seen as a great man and a great Michiganian, in 1938 he was a politician who had as many enemies as he had friends and who presided over a weak economy. Fitzgerald served as governor for only a few months before he died and was succeeded by Luren D. Dickinson.

In many ways by this point the election of governors was not nearly as important as it had been prior to the depression. Relief and recovery programs were designed and run by federal officials. While a governor on good terms with the national administration might add a bit to the state's share of these resources, there was no way Michigan could or would opt out of any of the major federal programs in a meaningful way or be excluded from them. Initiative and power had shifted to Washington. The outbreak of war in 1939 brought another factor into play as the attention of the president and the nation's leaders shifted to the international scene.

One bright spot for Michiganians during the dark days of the depression was the Tigers, who fielded some of their best teams ever during the 1930s. In 1934 they went 101–53, the best winning percentage in team history, and hit .300 as a team while winning the American League pennant. Future Hall of Famers Goose Goslin, Mickey Cochrane, Hank Greenberg, and Charlie Gehringer, from Fowlerville, were the stars on a team that also included shortstop Billy Rogell, who went on to be elected several times to the Detroit City Council. In 1935 the Tigers won their first World Series, and they won yet another pennant in

1940. Radio, one of the new consumer products that had fueled the lost prosperity of the 1920s, brought the Tigers to fans across the state who could not afford to attend the games at Navin Field.

Radio also brought another Michiganian to prominence and put him in the center of controversy. Rev. Charles Coughlin, pastor of the Shrine of the Little Flower, a Roman Catholic parish in Royal Oak, developed a national following as "the radio priest." Coughlin had been sent to Royal Oak in 1926 by Detroit bishop Michael Gallagher to found a new parish in the growing suburbs of Detroit. That same year he began a series of sermons and then children's programs on the new medium of radio. In 1930 he began to discuss his views on political and economic issues and quickly attracted a national audience. He was initially harshly critical of communism, internationalism, and the policies of Herbert Hoover, combining populist economics with the social teachings of the papal encyclicals. He was also initially a strong supporter of Franklin Roosevelt and the New Deal, but eventually broke with Roosevelt over monetary policy, favoring instead policies to promote high inflation. When CBS Radio, which carried his show nationally, dropped him in 1934 and NBC refused to even negotiate with him he organized his own network, the National Union for Social Justice. The union had millions of members across the country and published a magazine, *Social Justice*. Coughlin became increasingly vitriolic in his attacks on Roosevelt and his programs became increasingly anti-Semitic in tone. Coughlin's audience was constantly shifting as his message and the way he presented it alternatively drew in and then alienated people.

While he enjoyed the support and protection of Bishop Gallagher, there was growing opposition within the Catholic Church to his extreme views and vicious attacks on Roosevelt and other public figures. When Gallagher's successor, Edward Mooney, arrived in Detroit in 1937, Father Coughlin was on the short list of major problems facing the new Archbishop. Mooney quickly appointed an ecclesiastical censor for Coughlin's radio speeches and columns in *Social Justice*. He withheld his imprimatur from several articles in the magazine that attacked the Congress of Industrial Organizations (CIO) and publicly stated that Catholics could join the CIO, contrary to the view expressed by Coughlin. The "radio priest" and the Archbishop were frequently at odds in the press. Coughlin's followers sent petitions to Rome on his behalf, and he had strong supporters in several influential national Catholic publications that made it difficult for Mooney to control him. In 1940, however, Mooney did act decisively and Coughlin was forced off the air and removed from open involvement with *Social Justice*. He returned to being only the pastor of Little Flower, quietly retiring in 1966.[24]

Coughlin's increasing anti-Semitism and harsh denunciation of Roosevelt were hard for the Archbishop to ignore because of the rise of Nazism under Adolf Hitler and the outbreak of war in Europe. With the fall of France during the summer of 1940 increasingly urgent calls for military preparedness dominated the national political scene. President Roosevelt accepted nomination for an unprecedented third term in the face of the great crisis. More importantly, the Republicans nominated Wendell Wilkie, who supported many of Roosevelt's policies which were designed to assist the British, over Senator Arthur Vandenberg of Grand Rapids, who was strongly opposed to any steps that might draw the United States into the war.

Even before the election in the fall of 1940 the nation began to shift gears and move to restructure the economy for war. The National Defense Advisory Commission was established to coordinate the massive effort that would be involved. General Motors president William S. Knudsen was selected as director of the commission's critical industrial production division. From this position, and later as head of the Office of Production Management, Knudsen played a key role in the retooling of America as its vast industrial capacity, underutilized for a decade, was reactivated and increasingly focused on war production.

One of the underappreciated aspects of Michigan's automobile industry is the extent to which it rests on a base of machine tool skills and machinery of great flexibility. While the assembly line has attracted the most attention and has captured the popular imagination about the nature of the industry, it was the auto industry's ability to mass produce myriad components, manage the continuing innovations that characterized the industry, and coordinate the assembly of very complex products that allowed it to adjust to the needs of the war effort without major disruption. Retooling to produce new products—very large, very complex products—was what the industry did on a regular basis.

When Congress established a draft in September 1940 and began the expansion of the armed forces, the persistent national unemployment problem was finally beaten. Some 670,000 Michiganians served in the armed forces during the war, but several times as many—men and women, white, black, and Hispanic—made equally important contributions to the war effort in the factories that armed the Allies. Michigan's factories quickly moved from operating at minimal levels, if at all, to full-scale production of a vast array of military vehicles, weapons, and equipment.

The retooling of the Michigan auto industry at the onset of the Second World War is one of the great stories in industrial history. Michigan's industrial core, including industries both related and unrelated to auto production, earned the title of the Arsenal of Democracy because of the range and mass of materiel it produced. This transformation not only provided jobs for those who had been out of work for so long, but once again made Michigan a destination for southern whites, largely from Kentucky and Tennessee, and for blacks who came to work in the new defense plants. Detroit gained nearly a half million residents between 1940 and 1943, 80 percent of whom were from out of state.

The influx of such a diverse mix of new residents was not without its problems. Relations between the races had long been tense in Detroit and were exacerbated by housing shortages in the traditionally black areas of the city. In 1925 when a white mob protested Dr. Ossian Sweet and his family moving into a white neighborhood, rocks thrown at the house resulted in shots that killed two whites. The resulting trial attracted national attention as Clarence Darrow won an acquittal for the defendants, including Dr. Sweet, on first-degree murder charges by arguing their right to defend their property and their own lives.

The migration into Detroit in the early 1940s of southern whites and blacks in large numbers quickly brought these tensions to the surface. In 1942 whites rioted to force blacks to abandon the Sojourner Truth Project, a federal housing project for blacks built in a previously white part of the city. There were other small racial incidents throughout the city, most so minor and isolated that they failed to attract widespread attention.

On June 20, 1943, a series of fights between whites and blacks broke out on Belle Isle and quickly escalated into a major riot throughout the city. All of the tensions and animosity that had been building for several years erupted in an ugly, violent riot that terrorized large parts of the city and attracted national attention to the poor state of race relations in Detroit. The governor flew back to the state from a governors' conference in Ohio and after some confusion requested federal troops to help restore order in the city. When order was finally restored, thirty-four were dead, twenty-five of whom were black, hundreds were injured, and property damage totaled $2 million. Production in the defense plants had fallen by 40 percent during the riots. The riot gave way to a rancorous debate over who was responsible and what could be done to avoid such a conflict in the future.[25]

The auto companies played a central and highly visible role in Michigan's transformation into an arsenal, not only because of their size but also because of the flexibility their strong machine tool base gave them. No industry had done more to institutionalize major changes in its products and the requisite retooling for their production than the auto industry. The industry's leaders overcame their strong initial reluctance to convert the industry wholesale to war production, a reluctance based on both a desire to do what they were comfortable with—make cars—and their memories of how the infant industry had been left in the lurch by the government when the First World War had ended. By 1940 the economy had recovered to the point where the market for automobiles was reemerging, and industry leaders were reluctant to abandon that and convert their plants to war production.

Knudsen played a key role balancing the industry's concerns and the government's needs, a balancing act that continued throughout the war.[26] The reluctance of the industry was largely overcome by the adoption of a policy whereby the federal government built the new

31

plants, which were then operated by the auto manufacturers, who had not committed their capital to the project and thus had far less to lose if the war and its demand for material was short.

Between Hitler's invasion of Poland in September 1939 and the end of the war in August 1945, the auto industry alone produced nearly $50 billion in war material, the largest part of it in Michigan. Of this, some 30 percent was vehicles and another 13 percent tanks. Nearly 40 percent was aircraft and aircraft parts, with the balance in a range of products, including marine equipment, guns, artillery, and ammunition.[27] The ability of the auto industry to manufacture highly complex products in volume was critical.

General Motors's Saginaw Steering Gear Division (SSG) is a good example. Steering Gear took its name from its location, Saginaw, and its main product, steering gears, but these were very complex mechanical constructions, requiring many parts machined to tight tolerances. The division had a tradition of product innovation and a corps of highly skilled machinists and engineers, many of whom were working on WPA projects because of layoffs when the war began in Europe. Late in 1937 the division was asked if machine guns could be manufactured using the same techniques that were used for steering gears. By March 1938 SSG had submitted a plan for the production of twenty-five thousand M1919A4 machine guns annually.

Although many in the army were skeptical about the possibility of producing the weapon in such quantity, lack of funding was the reason nothing was done until June 1940, when an order was finally placed. SSG was to deliver 280 machine guns by March 1942. Steel was set for a new plant building in November 1940, and by March 1941 516 people were at work, producing the first finished gun by the 27th of that month. More workers were added as fast as there was machinery for them to operate. By the March 1942 delivery date more than 28,000, rather than 280, machine guns had been delivered, at less than a quarter of the estimated price per gun. By the end of the war the guns were being produced for less than $55 each, as opposed to an initial estimate of $657. All in all, the division produced more than 400,000 machine guns, 517,000 carbines, and 13.5 millions rounds of ammunition. This was in addition to producing replacement parts for prewar vehicles and developing hydraulic steering gears for a variety of military vehicles, from troop transports to amphibious ducks. Employment increased from about 1,200 in December 1940 to a peak of some 9,300 in 1943.[28]

Throughout the auto industry and the state's other industries there were many similar stories. Chrysler took responsibility for manufacturing tanks in the summer of 1940 and by September 1941 the first of twenty-five thousand tanks were rolling off the assembly line at the Chrysler Tank Arsenal in Macomb County. General Motors also produced tanks at a plant in

Grand Blanc built for that purpose. Packard shifted to the production of aircraft engines. Across the state factories reopened, people went back to work at good wages, and new plants were built, and more labor was needed than Michigan could provide.

The great symbol of the wartime transformation of Michigan's industrial base and its contribution to the war effort was Ford's Willow Run bomber plant in Washtenaw County. Designed by Albert Kahn, the plant cost $100 million and took almost a year and a half to build. Its demand for labor led to the construction of a highway to allow workers from Detroit to commute and the construction of a village to house workers who came not only from Michigan, but from all over the country. Even with the additional housing the village provided, Ypsilanti, the nearest community, was overwhelmed by the demand for housing by workers moving to the community from other parts of Michigan and from the South, especially from Tennessee and Kentucky.

When production of the B-24 began in September 1942 there were many problems, due to difficulties in the recruiting and training of workers and to constant design changes by the military. Charles E. Sorenson, the executive in charge, and Ford engineers solved the problems and by the end of 1943 the production goal of one plane per hour was exceeded. In all, more than 8,500 B-24 Liberator bombers were produced at Willow Run and flown from the adjacent airfield to the European Theater, where they were the backbone of the strategic bombing campaign.

While the southeastern corner of Michigan, the heart of the auto industry, achieved fame as the Arsenal of Democracy, other industrial areas in Michigan, especially Grand Rapids, also played an important role in the war effort. As in the case of the auto industry, some of the products produced in Grand Rapids were familiar, as with American Seating's manufacture of metal chairs for the armed forces and Metal Office Furniture's (now Steelcase) production of steel bunks, desks, chairs, and tables—including the table on which the Japanese surrender was signed. Other firms applied their workers' skills to a broader range of products, as with Hayes Manufacturing, which switched from production of auto bodies to manufacture of truck cabs, torpedo casings, parachutes, and bomb fins. Irwin Furniture and Pedersen Arms Manufacturing combined to produce M1 carbines, and the Nash-Kelvinator refrigerator plant switched to the manufacture of R6 helicopters. Grand Rapids' smaller firms were concerned that they were unable to compete for defense work, so they formed Grand Rapids Industries to coordinate their efforts and bid on projects too large for any one firm. Grand Rapids Industries was not only successful but became a model the War Department urged other communities to adopt.[29]

While there were few army or navy bases in Michigan during the war, Grand Rapids was the site of the Army Air Forces Weather school, which took over the Pantlind and Rowe Hotels as barracks and used the civic center as a huge lecture hall.

The demands of the defense plants for labor opened up opportunities for women. Some 200,000 women worked in defense plants in jobs traditionally held by men or created by the conversion to military production. The transition was rapid. There were only 300 women production workers at Ford's Highland Park plant in 1942, but by the next year that number had risen to 4,500. No women worked at Ford's Rouge plant or GM's Detroit Cadillac plant in the spring of 1942. By March of 1943 there were 5,000 women working at Rouge and 4,400 at Cadillac.[30] Rosie the Riveter and Winnie the Welder became cultural icons and symbols of women's contributions to the war effort. Only 20 percent of working women were in manufacturing in 1940, compared to 34 percent in 1944. Many had moved from other industries for the higher wages available in defense plants.[31]

War production brought the iron and copper mines of the Upper Peninsula back into operation and put the miners back to work. It also made the locks at Sault Ste. Marie critical to the war effort, and the Soo Locks became one of the most heavily fortified sites in the country, complete with antiaircraft guns and barrage balloons. The Ford plant in Kingsford that had made wooden bodies for station wagons was converted to manufacturing gliders, which were also manufactured in Grand Rapids. In Battle Creek, workers at Kellogg produced K rations. Many Michigan industries were able to retool and refocus their efforts on war production, and the state, with roughly 4 percent of the nation's population, received more than 10 percent of major defense contracts. Many Michigan corporations received the "Army-Navy E Award" for their accomplishments in meeting production goals and timetables. A look at the list of those who received this award reveals just how widespread was the conversion of the economy and the resulting return of prosperity. Fifty-three separate firms from Detroit were represented, as were the Calumet and Hecla Consolidated Copper Company from Calumet, Ford Motor Company's Iron Mountain (actually Kingsford) glider plant, the Besser Manufacturing Company of Alpena, and hundreds of others from all areas of the state.[32]

Less well known than Michigan's role as the industrial "Arsenal of Democracy" was the resurgence of agriculture in the state during the war. While the number of farms and the farm population had begun to decline in the early 1920s, half of the land in Michigan was still classified as farm- and cropland in 1940. The state was among the leading producers of dairy and livestock products, feed grains, field vegetables, and fruit. Although farmworkers could qualify for draft deferments, labor was the main obstacle to increased agricultural production. Defense work paid very well and attracted many from rural areas. Others enlisted in the armed forces despite the availability of deferments. Beginning in the fall of 1943 the government used German and Italian prisoners of war in agriculture and in food-processing plants. The army established a reception center and base camp at Fort Custer near Battle Creek. Most of the work was done by POWs sent to branch camps, which were often tent villages, although some were former CCC camps and had barracks and other buildings. At least twenty-five such camps operated in Michigan in 1944–45, from Dundee and Blissfield in the southeastern Lower Peninsula to Au Train and Wetmore in the Upper Peninsula.[33]

There was more to life in Michigan during the war years than defense work and farm life. It was a time of saying goodbye to family and friends as they went off to fight and participating in scrap drives and bond drives and a variety of patriotic programs to support the war effort. Ronald Jager, who grew up on a farm in Missaukee County during the war, remembers the scrap drives.

> All the farms in our neighborhood had riches to contribute to the national harvest: first from the dump behind the house, then from the piles beyond the barn and beside the stone pile, where lay many a broken hunk of cast iron and various abandoned implements of rusty steel. They had accumulated and moldered through the years, and now would be reborn as guns and tanks. . . . After the heavy metals came the lighter stuff: small steel, aluminum, rubber, tin, paper. Our school put on scrap drives and different grades competed against one another. We took packages of newspapers and old rusty pails full of bits of scrap on the bus, and we weighed the iron and heaved it on the pile west of school. . . . You could get admitted to a basketball game for fifteen pounds of scrap iron or twenty-five pounds of paper.[34]

Rationing and food shortages were also a part of the war experience for Michiganians. Gasoline, tires, butter, sugar, and a number of other staples once considered necessities were rationed for civilian use. Yet not everything during the war was somber: the Tigers won the pennant in 1940 and came close in 1944, powered by the stellar pitching of Dizzy Trout, with twenty-seven wins, and Detroit-born Hal Newhouser, who won twenty-nine games. The following year Newhouser won twenty-five and his second MVP award as the Tigers, buoyed by the return from the service of slugger Hank Greenberg in midseason, won the pennant and the World Series.

The flood of war orders and the expansion of the military brought full employment and economic prosperity back to Michigan rapidly after 1940. Factories reopened and new defense plants were built to arm the United States and its allies. Michigan once again became a destination for those pursuing the American dream. After the war, when the troops returned, the Cold War, the GI Bill, and the pent up demand for consumer goods following years of depression followed by war rationing kept industrial production and employment high. The UAW and other unions had secured a place at the bargaining table to represent the needs and interests of Michigan's industrial workforce. Economic security was no longer merely a dream or a memory for working Michiganians; it had once again become their reality. The dream of the good life and economic security had been reclaimed.

NOTES

1. There is a vast amount of literature available on this transformation: good introductions can be found in Frederick Lewis Allen, *Only Yesterday: An Informal History of the 1920's* (N.Y.: Harper Brothers, 1931) and George E. Mowry, ed., *The Twenties: Fords, Flappers and Fanatics* (Englewood Cliffs, N.J.: Prentice-Hall, 1963).

2. On the impact of the rapid expansion of the automobile industry on Flint see Ronald Edsforth, *Class Conflict and Cultural Consensus: The Making of a Mass Consumer Society in Flint, Michigan* (New Brunswick, N.J.: Rutgers University Press, 1987).

3. Willis F. Dunbar and George S. May, *Michigan: A History of the Wolverine State,* rev. ed. (Grand Rapids: William B. Eerdmans Publishing Co., 1980).

4. *A Half Century Ago: Michigan in the Great Depression* (East Lansing: n.p., 1980).

5. Quoted in Philip A. Korth, "Boom, Bust & Bombs: The Michigan Economy," in Richard J. Hathaway, ed., *Michigan: Visions of Our Past* (East Lansing: Michigan State University Press, 1987), 226. See also Nora Faires, "Transition and Turmoil: Social and Political Developments in Michigan, 1917–145," in ibid., 201–17.

6. Quoted in Sidney Fine, *Frank Murphy: The Detroit Years* (Ann Arbor: University of Michigan Press, 1975), 226.

7. Ibid., 226ff.

8. On Murphy's efforts to fight unemployment and its consequences in Detroit see: J. Woodford Howard Jr., *Mr. Justice Murphy: A Political Biography* (Princeton, N.J.: Princeton University Press, 1968) and Fine, *Frank Murphy: The Detroit Years.* Fine elegantly summarizes his other two volumes on Murphy in *Frank Murphy: A Michigan Life,* 1984 Burton Lecture (Ann Arbor: Historical Society of Michigan, 1985).

9. Charles A. Symon, *We Can Do It! A History of the Civilian Conservation Corps in Michigan, 1933–1942* (Escanaba, Mich.: Richards Printing, 1983), 2.

10. Richard H. Harms, "Paid in Scrip," *Michigan History Magazine* 75, no. 1 (January 1991): 37–43; Gordon L. Olson, *Grand Rapids Sampler* (Grand Rapids, Mich.: Grand Rapids Historical Commission, 1992), 147–70.

11. "Our Readers Remember Banking and Trust," *Michigan History Magazine* 66, no. 1 (1982): 37.

12. Doris B. McLaughlin, "Putting Michigan Back to Work: Bill Haber Remembers the 1930s," *Michigan History Magazine* 66, no. 1 (1982): 30–35; Louise V. Armstrong, *We Too Are the People* (Boston: Little, Brown and Company, 1938; reprint, New York: Arno, 1971).

13. "Hard Times and the WPA," *Copper Country Anthem* 4, no. 4 (1979): 7.

14. Ibid.

15. Ibid.

16. Arthur W. Thurner, *Strangers and Sojourners: A History of Michigan's Keweenaw Peninsula* (Detroit: Wayne State University Press, 1994), 226–57

17. Christine Nelson Ruby, "Art for the Millions: Government Art During the Depression," *Michigan History Magazine* 66, no. 1 (1982): 17–20.
18. Harold Richards, quoted in "Hard Times and the WPA," 10.
19. James Van Vulpen, *On Wings of Progress: The Story of the Kent County International Airport* (Grand Rapids, Mich.: Grand Rapids Historical Commission, 1989), 35–44.
20. Symon, *We Can Do It!*, passim.
21. Ibid.
22. Elizabeth Wahtola, quoted in "Hard Times and the WPA," 9.
23. The definitive historical account of the strike remains Sidney Fine, *Sit Down: The General Motors Strike of 1936–1937* (Ann Arbor: University of Michigan Press, 1969).
24. Leslie Woodcock Tentler, *Seasons of Grace: A History of the Catholic Archdiocese of Detroit* (Detroit: Wayne State University Press, 1990), 318–42, passim.
25. "Michigan Goes to War: Detroit's 1943 Riot," *Michigan History Magazine* 77, no. 3 (1993): 34–39; Dunbar and May, *Michigan*, 618–21.
26. Larry Lankton, "Autos to Armaments: Detroit Becomes the Arsenal of Democracy," *Michigan History Magazine* 75, no. 6 (1991): 42–49; Alan Clive, *State of War: Michigan in World War II* (Ann Arbor: University of Michigan Press, 1979); Richard H. Harms and Robert Viol, *Grand Rapids Goes to War: The 1940s Homefront* (Grand Rapids, Mich.: Grand Rapids Historical Society, 1993).
27. Dunbar and May, *Michigan*, 615.
28. Plant One History Committee, *From Gaslight to Starlight: A History of Plant One Saginaw Steering Gear* (n.p., n.d.), 18–27.
29. Gordon L. Olson, Grand Rapids: *A City Renewed* (Grand Rapids, Mich.: Grand Rapids Historical Commission, 1996), 2.
30. Nancy Gabin, "The Hand that Rocks the Cradle Can Build Tractors, Too," *Michigan History Magazine* 76, no. 2 (1992): 12–21.
31. Ibid., 19.
32. Tiffany B. Dziurman, "Awarding Excellence," *Michigan History Magazine* 78, no. 4 (1994): 22–23.
33. Duane Ernest Miller, "Barbed-Wire Farm Laborers: Michigan's Prisoner of War Experience during World War II," *Michigan History Magazine* 73, no. 4 (1989): 12–17.
34. Ronald Jager, "Eighty Acres," *Michigan History Magazine* 74, no. 6 (1990): 16–17.

ROY STRYKER,
THE FARM SECURITY ADMINISTRATION,
AND THE OFFICE OF WAR INFORMATION

Constance B. Schulz

The photographs that have come to symbolize in the minds of many Americans the essence of American experience during the Great Depression and the Second World War were created and gathered by an agency with much broader goals than simple historic remembrance. They have been so inextricably attached to the name of the agency that many who use them forget that the Farm Security Administration (FSA), originally called the Resettlement Administration (RA), did not begin as a documentary photographic project. Economic reformers conceived the RA during the first New Deal as a creative attempt to address one of the most intractable problems of the depression—the economic crisis of the rural poor, particularly the small landowners and tenant farmers, many of whom had been in a state of economic decline since the early 1920s.

The man appointed to find a solution to this problem, Rexford Guy Tugwell (1891–1979), was one of several charismatic, energetic, and intellectual figures drawn to Franklin D. Roosevelt during his first campaign for the presidency. These intellectuals became known collectively as the "Brains Trust." Tugwell was the son of a cattle dealer and a schoolteacher in Buffalo, New York. After graduating from the University of Pennsylvania's Wharton School in Philadelphia, he taught economics there and at the University of Washington, then managed the American University Union in Paris for two years before beginning his long career as a popular teacher of economics at Columbia University in New York in 1920. At Columbia, Tugwell embarked on an ambitious project to create a comprehensive textbook on *American Economic Life* for his section of the freshman course on "Contemporary Civilization." Tugwell had pioneered in using visual images in his classroom to teach his students about the realities of economic life. Believing that photographic illustrations in a textbook could serve the same function of bringing economic principals to life, he hired a young graduate assistant, Roy Emerson Stryker (1893–1973), to search for visual images to document the book's detailed descriptions of American economic activities.

A reformer who believed in the power of economic planning and experimentation to improve society, Tugwell visited the Soviet Union in 1927 and found much to admire in the successful collectivization of agriculture. An advisor on farm policy for Democratic governor Al Smith of New York during the 1920s, he also served as an advisor to Franklin D. Roosevelt when he became governor of New York, and continued in that role during Roosevelt's 1932 presidential campaign. After the election Roosevelt invited him to join the staff of Secretary of Agriculture Henry A. Wallace, where Tugwell eventually rose to the position of undersecretary of agriculture. When early in 1935 it became clear that the Agricultural Adjustment Act's attempts to raise farm prices by taking land out of production in order to reduce crop surpluses had displaced thousands of small farm owners, tenant farmers, and farm laborers, Roosevelt created a new executive agency, the Resettlement Administration (RA), to find an economic role for the poorest third of the nation's farmers. Tugwell was named as its director.

Tugwell initiated a series of aggressive economic experiments at the RA based on his belief that many of these farmers would never successfully return to operating individual small farms. For the migrant farm laborer, he set out to develop government-sponsored housing camps with good sanitation and low rents. For those on worn-out land, he proposed relocation to communal farms sited in areas with better soil, where cooperative labor could produce a sustainable agricultural economy. Realizing that these programs would be controversial, Tugwell determined to counter criticism and win over opponents by establishing an "Information Division" that would extol the accomplishments of the RA to a skeptical public and Congress. Drawing on his experiences as a teacher at Columbia, he decided that the publications of the Information Division should include extensive photographic documentation of the agency's work and the problems it was attempting to solve. To head the "Historical Section" created to carry out this task he called on his former Columbia student and research collaborator, Roy Emerson Stryker.[1]

When he came to Washington, D.C., in July 1935, Roy Stryker, at forty-two, was at a crossroads in his own career. Born in Kansas, raised in Colorado by a radical Populist father who, his son remembered, prayed loudly, "Please God, damn the bankers of Wall Street, damn the railroads, and double damn the Standard Oil Company," Stryker had been educated at the Colorado School of Mines, had served as a foot soldier in the first World War, and had made his way after the war to the East Coast for graduate study in agricultural economics at Columbia University. There, under Tugwell's tutelage, he discovered in himself a gift for teaching and a love of photography, but no particular bent for scholarship; he never finished his Ph.D. degree.

As a teacher, Stryker embraced wholeheartedly another faculty member's innovative technique of taking students into the streets of New York to see firsthand in banks and slums the economic and social conditions under which ordinary citizens lived and worked. In this "laboratory course" in "Contemporary Civilization" Stryker taught students how to observe carefully and record telling details. Working on the three editions of *American Economic Life* for Tugwell brought Stryker into close contact with the reformer photographer Lewis Hine, whose images formed the majority of illustrations in the two editions published by Harcourt Brace and Company, and with Margaret Bourke-White. In the process, he became, in the words of Dorothea Lange, "a natural picture-lover . . . [who] saves pictures like some people save string."[2]

All of these experiences were part of the intellectual and pedagogical "baggage" that Stryker brought with him to his new position. His vaguely defined "Historical Section" responsibility to "direct the activities of investigators, photographers, economists, sociologists and statisticians engaged in the accumulation and compilation of reports. . ., statistics, photographic material, . . . to make accurate descriptions of the various . . . phases of the Resettlement Administration, particularly with regard to the historical, sociological and economic aspects of the several programs" provided a great deal of leeway within which Stryker could teach and use his love of photography toward the accomplishment of significant agricultural reform.[3]

Stryker knew something about photographs but almost nothing about the technical side of photography. Accordingly, he took with him from New York to Washington Arthur Rothstein, a premedical student from Stryker's "Contemporary Civilization" laboratory course who had done much of the copy photography and laboratory work for a project Stryker had started at Columbia to document American agriculture. Stryker assigned Rothstein to set up a darkroom and begin photographing the activities of the RA. Within a short time, the head of the RA Information Division, J. Franklin Carter (1897–1967), restructured the agency so that all of its photographic work would fall under the direction of Stryker's "Historical Section," and assigned two other photographers, Carl Mydans and Walker Evans, to his direction.

Mydans had worked as a journalist and adopted the 35 mm "miniature" camera as a tool whose small size enabled him to achieve remarkably intimate portraits of his subjects. Evans was an artist as well as a photographer, and already had developed the unique vision that would make him perhaps the best known of the FSA photographers. Where Tugwell and Lewis Hine had taught Stryker to understand photographs as documents that capture reality and have the power to make people see social problems in a new light, Mydans and Evans taught him to understand the importance of the visual integrity and artistic qualities of photographic images.

Within a short time, the "Section" expanded to five photographers with the addition of artist Ben Shahn and photographer-reformer Dorothea Lange. Lange had been hired by University of California economics professor Paul Taylor (whom she later married) to take field photographs to illustrate a report on the terrible agricultural conditions in central California. Her uncompromising yet sympathetic images of the West Coast migrant workers fell into Tugwell's hands, and Tugwell brought her work to Stryker's attention. Unlike that of the others, initially her photographic work centered on the West Coast.

During the life of the agency, Stryker hired forty-four photographers, but the bulk of the photographs in the file are the work of fifteen men and women, of whom four (Russell Lee, Arthur Rothstein, John Vachon, and Arthur Siegel) completed one or more shooting assignments in Michigan. Like many small government offices, the Historical Section had an uncertain budget, which sometimes reduced Stryker to one or two salaried staff photographers. He supplemented the work of his full-time staff by hiring others on a freelance basis or for a short term to complete a particular assignment. Arthur Siegel probably carried out much of his work in Michigan under the latter type of arrangement.[4]

Resettlement Administration policies, particularly the construction of cooperative farms, did arouse the controversy that Tugwell expected, and by 1937 the RA had drawn congressional attention and ire. Early in that year Tugwell resigned, and his agency, including the Historical Section, became part of the Department of Agriculture. In July 1937 Congress passed a Farm Security Act which renamed the agency the Farm Security Administration (FSA). By then Stryker had become a seasoned bureaucrat, defending the work of his staff to congressional critics, and actively promoting the use of photographs from the files in exhibitions and their publication in newspapers, the new pictorial magazines *Life* and *Look*, and government agency reports.[5]

The work of the RA/FSA took place in two phases and locations: at the main offices in Washington, D.C., and out in the field in the forty-eight states. At his headquarters in the old Department of Agriculture Building, Stryker, his secretaries, the darkroom and supply room, and the growing file of images provided an energetic center of operations. Photographers hired by Stryker were briefed on their assignments; given cameras, film, and flashbulbs; and sent out into the field with a series of general instructions that came to be known as "shooting scripts." The existence of these scripts has recently formed the basis for a considerable body of criticism that the photographs provide an inaccurate portrayal of reality. In this view, the images were and are "propaganda," manipulated and directed from headquarters with a conscious agenda of justifying radical social policies by portraying rural Americans in a particular way. Other critics argue that the photographers who used the scripts, intent on making personal artistic statements, further distorted the record they created by following—or attempting to set—the fashions of "art."[6]

42

The photographers, however, remembered the "shooting scripts" as an extension of Roy Stryker's instinctive behavior as a teacher. Every one of the photographers interviewed for the Archives of American Art oral history project on the FSA eventually gravitated to a discussion of Roy's insistence that they learn as much as they could about the people and the places they were photographing. Was Arthur Rothstein's assignment to go to the Great Plains to document cattle farming under drought conditions? Stryker would sit him down in the Washington office, talk for several hours about the cattle business, send him on his travels with books about the subject, and bombard him with letters from headquarters that raised questions and proposed potential images that might help others see vicariously how things actually were. Just as he had taken his Columbia students into the streets of New York and insisted that they look at the gritty details of the economy in action, Stryker wanted to teach his photographers how to see the world around them. To do that, he believed, it was necessary to understand the larger forces at work in a community or an industry, to have a grasp both of the whole picture and of the myriad details that gave it coherence and integrity. His shooting scripts were reminders of the small things photographers needed to look for in order to capture that larger context. He wanted his photographers to focus not on a particular problem or family for itself, but to see it in the complex setting of the daily life of its community, or in the details of a landscape or a process.

The result of this approach was the growth at headquarters in Washington of a remarkable file of images. In contrast to later documentary photography projects, Roy's photographers were creating a resource, not looking for a story. As Arthur Rothstein described it from his later vantage point as a photographer and photographic editor for *Look*,

> All of the photography that I do now is designed for publication. Every picture that I take is taken with the idea that this picture is going to be printed somewhere. . . . When I worked for the Resettlement Administration . . . , the pictures were not taken for publication. . . . They were taken as a historical record. The emphasis was on the quality of the photography as a means of getting across information and at the same time preserving a certain amount of artistic interpretation, using the fine arts aspect of the photographic medium to explain and show what life was like in that particular part of the country. . . . [At *Look*] the picture is a means to an end. In the case of the Resettlement Administration the picture *was* the end. . . . The idea was to get pictures in the file.[7]

The photographers sent most negatives back to the Washington lab for developing and printing. Roy Stryker reviewed the contact prints, making decisions about which to keep and which to "kill," often writing comments about each batch. He usually sent the contact prints and his comments back to the photographer in the field in care of the nearest local post office. The photographers then wrote captions for each image on file cards, using field notes written when the photos were taken. Sometimes photographers home in Washington between assignments came into the office to do this job. At least some of the photographers thought this was one of the weaker parts of the project, because captions were written out of context. As Rothstein explained, "If we had had writer-photographer teams . . . one to record things in words and the other to record things in pictures . . . perhaps the results would have been more meaningful. . . . I find going through the files that a lot of pictures have very scanty captions, and that the captions are not really indicative of everything that went on."[8] Finally, clerks copied the captions onto the back of the 8 x 10 photographs that went into the permanent file.

John Vachon, who was hired first as a "messenger," then assigned to copy captions, and eventually put in charge of the file, developed the system for their retrieval:

> I organized them on the basis that there were forty-eight states, so all pictures from Alabama went under "Alabama," with classifications under that which tended to keep what would be picture stories—things all taken in the same town, or of the same family, together with a title. There would be the miscellaneous things left over, which I would call 'Small Town Scenes,' or 'General Rural Areas,' or something like that. There was nothing similar to the Dewey Decimal System or any scientific kind of classification.[9]

Newspaper and magazine editors, government researchers needing illustrations for reports, and agencies planning exhibits publicizing the successes of their work turned to this file for photographic materials.

The photographers in the field were thus pretty thoroughly divorced from the use of their images. The far-flung nature of their assignments would have made it difficult for them to have played a larger role in their distribution. Briefed by Stryker, equipped with "shooting scripts," kept in fairly constant touch with news from home by letters, telegrams, and an occasional visit in the field from Stryker, the photographers traveled by train, or drove their own cars, to remote rural locations in every state of the union to document agricultural life in America. Often they were on the road for months at a time. Stryker expected them to keep accurate logs of mileage and records of expenses, to send back a steady flow of negatives and captioned contact prints, and to be ready to change their itinerary on short notice from headquarters if an opportunity or a contact for good photography opened up. Russell Lee preferred to do his own lab work. After several days of shooting, he would stop for an extra day in a local hotel, where he would convert his bathroom into a darkroom.

When in a particular region, the photographers were often assigned to respond to requests from area supervisors to document local RA/FSA project activities. Most of the time, the photographers regarded these "publicity" assignments as routine and uninspiring, and the local agents' ideas of what they should photograph as unimaginative. Their letters to Stryker, responding to these and other assignments, are a fascinating combination of routine requests for supplies of film and flashbulbs, complaints about the weather and traveling conditions, and perceptive and thoughtful descriptions of places and people.[10]

Before 1939, the regions to which the photographers traveled were predominantly rural, and most of the work that the Section did was for its own agency, the FSA. Late in 1936 Stryker had a series of conversations with Robert Lynd, the sociologist whose *Middletown: A Study in American Culture* (1929) had directed scholarly attention to the cultural life of small communities. These conversations stimulated Stryker to add to his shooting scripts lists of the kinds of things his photographers should look for in order to document the importance of the rural towns that served the farming population. Several subsequent field trip assignments, especially those of Russell Lee, were town community studies, but these photographs were still closely connected to the agrarian mission of the RA and FSA as a whole.

Two factors contributed to a change in this concentration on rural life, however, and the images in the file began to take on a new direction. The first factor was internal to the FSA: a severe budget cut in late 1937 and early 1938 reduced the Historical Section staff and left Stryker scrambling for resources. In part he found financial support to keep his photographers in the field through routine photographic work for FSA's parent agency, the Department of Agriculture. The Section's reputation for fine photography also attracted other agencies willing to contract with Stryker for the services of his FSA photographers. Most notable of these in 1937–38 was the Department of Public Health. Thus began a practice that increased substantially in the coming years.[11]

The second factor that precipitated change in the work of the photographers was the beginning of the war in Europe. Wartime demands, combined with the lessening of drought conditions in the Midwest, began to bring prosperity to farmers. Returning prosperity redirected much federal government concern away from solving agricultural problems and toward providing the resources for the Allied struggle against Hitler's aggressive military and economic strategies. Increasingly, other government agencies willing to pay the Historical Section for its photographic services included those involved with preparations for war. The images in the file reflect the gradual shift of shooting assignments toward plant construction, the lives of workers in the hastily constructed trailer camps and new residential neighborhoods, and the tasks undertaken in aircraft factories and shipyards or in railyards and harbors bustling to meet wartime shipment deadlines. Stryker wrote to photographer Jack Delano early in 1941, "It is important that we keep our finger in defense activities the way the whole world is moving now. . . . I am determined that we are not going to find ourselves liquidated because we got on the wrong wagon."[12]

With a shift in subject matter came a subtle change in perspective. Images shot for the file increasingly focused on celebration of "the American habit" of hard work, cheerfulness, and dependability and on "affirming photographs": rich rolling fields of ripening grain as opposed to the stark, raw soil of eroded cotton fields; hardworking, well-dressed war workers and their families as opposed to the destitute, sometimes pathetic, but often plucky and proud "poorest third of a nation." Because of the role of Michigan industries in meeting wartime demands, it is no accident that much of the photography done in the state by Stryker's photographers came after 1939.

By the time America entered the war in earnest in 1941, the entire Farm Security Administration was in serious political as well as budgetary trouble. Congressional hearings criticizing FSA programs led to a transfer of the least controversial programs to other agencies, and to elimination of its budget in 1943. In 1946 it was officially disbanded. Stryker saw the end coming, and in late 1942 managed to arrange for the transfer of his photographic operations into a new agency for which he had been doing an increasing amount of contract work: the Office of War Information (OWI).

The OWI was created in July 1941 as the Office of Coordinator of Information, designed to prevent duplication in the growing number of government information and propaganda efforts. It was renamed in June 1942 and placed under the Office of Emergency Management. A wartime information agency could not afford Stryker or his photographers the same broad license to exercise their own judgment that they had enjoyed within FSA. Associate director of the OWI Milton Eisenhower was sympathetic; he and Stryker were old friends from the days when Eisenhower had served as chief of the Information Division of the Department of Agriculture. Nevertheless, in a short time Stryker once again began to fear for the survival of his agency in the face of political struggles within the Domestic Operations Branch of the OWI. Part of the agency believed a free society needed freely available information, even in wartime, but another faction argued for closer control over information as a wartime security measure. More importantly, discussions of disbursing the images among other domestic propaganda collections threatened the continued integrity of the photographic files.

Early in 1943 Stryker looked for a suitable home for the collection, and that fall he made arrangements with Archibald MacLeish, the Librarian of Congress, for the library to receive the collection intact. Between 1944 and 1946, when the files were physically transferred to the library, where they now reside, archivist Paul Vanderbilt reorganized them for use by library patrons. The complicated system of geographic and subject categories that he created was designed to make it possible for users seeking images on particular topics to find them without the assistance of the FSA/OWI staff members who had provided that service during the agency's lifetime. Before moving the photographs physically into this new order, Vanderbilt arranged for them to be microfilmed in their original order.[13]

This hastily arranged transfer, cobbled together during the pressures of wartime, preserved a collection that has become one of the treasures of the Library of Congress and of the nation. Moreover, the arrangement of the images adopted then has survived for more than half a century. A resurgence in interest in these images, both as fine art and as historical documentation, began in the 1970s. This study of the way in which Michigan was portrayed by the six photographers Stryker sent to the Upper and Lower Peninsulas between 1936 and 1943 is one of more than a dozen books that have focused on the images of particular states found within the file.

NOTES

1. On Tugwell and the Resettlement Administration, see Kenneth T. Jackson, ed., *Dictionary of American Biography*, Supplement 10, 1976–1980 (New York: Charles Scribner's Sons, 1995), 794–96; F. Jack Hurley, *Portrait of a Decade* (Baton Rouge: Louisiana State University Press, 1972), 17–36; and Carl Fleischhauer and Beverly Brannan, eds., *Documenting America, 1935–1943* (Berkeley: University of California Press, 1988), 2–3.

2. Archives of American Art, Smithsonian Institution, Richard Doud interview with Dorothea Lange, May 22, 1964, microfilm edition, p. 6. On Stryker's early career generally, see Hurley, *Portrait*, 3–16; Constance B. Schulz, *Bust to Boom: Documentary Photographs of Kansas, 1936–49* (Lawrence: University Press of Kansas, 1996), 31–33; and Fleischhauer and Brannan, *Documenting America*, 3–4.

3. Quoted in Hurley, *Portrait*, 36.

4. Archives of American Art, Smithsonian Institution, Richard Doud interviews with Carl Mydans (April 29, 1964), Arthur Rothstein (May 25, 1964), Dorothea Lange (May 22, 1964), and Roy Stryker (Oct. 17, 1963, June 13–14, 1964, and Jan. 23, 1965); Hurley, *Portrait*, 37–42; Fleischhauer and Brannan, *Documenting America*, appendix, 337.

5. Schulz, *Bust to Boom*, 32–33; Archives of American Art, Smithsonian Institution, interviews with Dorothea Lange and Roy Stryker.

6. For thoughtful criticism of the RA/FSA photographs, see especially James Curtis, *Mind's Eye, Mind's Truth: FSA Photography Reconsidered* (Philadelphia: Temple University Press, 1989); Maren Stange, *"Symbols of Ideal Life": Social Documentary Photograph in America, 1890–1950* (New York: Cambridge University Press, 1988); and Alan Trachtenberg, *Reading American Photographs: Images as History, Matthew Brady to Walker Evans* (New York: Hill and Wang, 1989).

7. Archives of American Art, Smithsonian Institution, Richard Doud interview with Arthur Rothstein, May 25, 1964, p. 30.

8. Ibid., 27.

9. Archives of American Art, Smithsonian Institution, Richard Doud interview with John Vachon, April 28, 1964, pp. 1–3.

10. Correspondence, Roy Stryker Papers, Photographic Archives, University of Louisville, cited from microfilm edition (Cambridge: Chadwyck-Healey Ltd., 1978–81).

11. Hurley, *Portrait*, 104–8.

12. Roy Stryker to Jack Delano, April 8, 1941, quoted in Fleischhauer and Brannan, *Documenting America*, 5.

13. See the discussion of these two systems on pages 00–00. See also Constance B. Schulz, *A South Carolina Album, 1936–1948: Photographs from the Farm Security Administration, Office of War Information, and Standard Oil of New Jersey Documentary Projects* (Columbia: University of South Carolina Press, 1992), 11–12; Schulz, *Bust to Boom*, 36–37; and Fleischhauer and Brannan, *Documenting America*, 5–7.

MICHIGAN REMEMBERED

PHOTOGRAPHS FROM THE
FARM SECURITY ADMINISTRATION AND THE
OFFICE OF WAR INFORMATION, 1936–1943

I

The Upper Peninsula, 1937 and 1941

Aug. 1941, Baraga County. The Upper Peninsula. John Vachon. USF34-63500-D

THE TWO FARM SECURITY ADMINISTRATION photographers who drove into the Upper
Peninsula in the summers of 1937 and 1941 were intelligent outsiders, both born in the
Midwest, but unfamiliar with the particular beauty and poverty of Michigan's northern rural
reaches. Russell Lee grew up in Illinois, and John Vachon in St. Paul, Minnesota. Although
they briefly recorded the lakeport townscapes of Hancock, Houghton, and L'Anse, where the
region's copper, iron ore, and lumber products were loaded onto Great Lakes vessels, for the
most part they photographed the interior landscapes of the westernmost areas of the Upper
Peninsula: Ontonagon, Houghton, Keweenaw, Baraga, and Iron Counties. Their photographs
speak eloquently both of the beauty of the region and of the hardships they saw around them.

Aug. 1941, Hancock and Houghton. The two largest towns of the Michigan copper range. John Vachon. USF34-63544-D

RUSSELL LEE WAS ON AN assignment to document the depression crisis of the "cut-over" district in northern Wisconsin and Michigan. Like many RA/FSA photographers, he spent part of his time recording the attempts by the Resettlement Administration to alleviate the worst of the impact of economic crisis on ordinary people. He also searched beyond the cheerful surroundings of such projects for direct evidence of hardship, and found rocky fields, muddy roads, and "single shackers" trying to eke out a living from the nearly barren soil where vast tracts of white pine had once dominated the landscape. More than a quarter of a century later he remembered vividly the conditions he found:

> It must have been probably the latter part of March, because I remember getting plenty of snow, but yet realizing that spring was there. The "cut-over" areas up there were so called because in the . . . late nineteenth century and to some extent the early part of the twentieth century, there had been terrific logging operations up there in the white pine especially.

Aug. 1941, L'Anse. John Vachon. USF34-63506-D

The white pine was just—well, it was beyond comprehension what they did have up there. . . . They just cut right through the forest of white pine trees, right straight, so that they could have the railroads. . . . There was just no effort at conservation or anything like that. They just went in, and cut it all, and it was as they call it, the cut-over land. A group of enterprising young real-estate people came . . . down into the Chicago area, and sold some people in the city down there some of this fine land, to go up and farm. . . . And this was all fine, except the pine land, invariably, is very shallow and sandy, and is not good for cultivation of any crop. So the "cut-over" people had an awful time up there. I was sent up there to get some pictures of the life of those people . . . , and what they had to do to solve their problems of life, or existence, which was more what it turned out to be.[1]

_____

1. Archives of American Art, Smithsonian Institution, Richard Doud interview with Russell Lee, June 1964, pp. 5–6.

Jan. 1937, Ironwood Homesteads. A garden community project of the U.S. Resettlement administration. View of the new houses. Russell Lee. USF34-15426-E

Apr. 1937, Hagerman Lake. A former lumber camp, now a camp for transients operated by the state of Michigan. The roads are so bad that it is necessary to haul supplies by mud sled for the last quarter mile. The camp has no telephone system and no resident doctor.
Russell Lee. USF34-10815-E

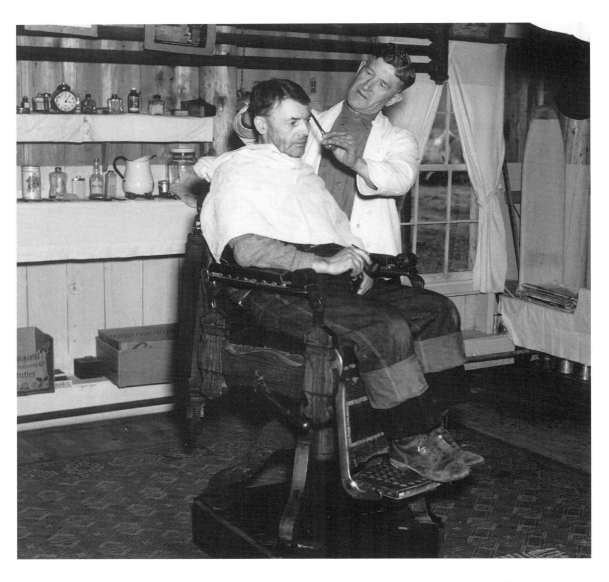

Apr. 1937, Hagerman Lake. A former lumber camp, now a camp for transients operated by the state of Michigan. Barber shop. Russell Lee. USF34-10817-D

Apr. 1937, Silk Lake (vicinity), Iron County. Barnyard of William Sharrard, a farmer on cut-over land. The portable sawmill on the sled was made from a model T Ford engine. Russell Lee. USF341-10827-B

May 1937, Silk Lake (vicinity), Iron County. Son of William Sharrard, a cut-over farmer, rolling a cigarette. Russell Lee. USF34-10965-E

May 1937, Silk Lake (vicinity), Iron County. One of William Sharrard's children in the doorway of their home. Russell Lee. USF34-10970-E

May 1937, Iron County. Removing stones from cut-over land on a stone boat.
Russell Lee. USF34-10941-E

May 1937, Iron River (vicinity). John Nygren, who lives alone in a shack.
Russell Lee. USF34-10806-E

May 1937, Iron County. John Bastia hanging up his laundry. He is a single shacker.
Russell Lee. USF34-10940-E

May 1937, Iron River (vicinity). Lon Allen and his son playing their fiddles to the tune of "The Arkansas traveler." The fiddle played by the son was made by him.
Russell Lee. USF34-10895-D

May 1937, Iron County. "Black Aleck" Dickinson and his dog, "Snoop." Russell Lee.
USF34-10901-D

May 1937, Gibbs City. Back porch on a washday. Russell Lee. USF34-10914-E

Apr. 1937, Gibbs City (vicinity). Child feeding a calf on a farm.
Russell Lee. USF34-10922-E

WHEN JOHN VACHON RETURNED TO the Upper Peninsula for the Farm Security Administration in August 1941, the soil quality had not improved but the economic outlook for the people who lived there had, as the beginnings of wartime production demands began to reach even into these abandoned coal, copper, and lumbering regions. In Trout Creek, lumber mills were again active; in the copper towns of Laurium and Franklin Mine, citizens were hopeful that dormant mines might be reopened. The successful harvest of a long summer brought the Finnish-American farm boys of Bruce's Crossing into the local beer parlor with pay in their pockets, where Vachon captured them in a brief moment of peace and companionship before many of them would be drafted into the armed forces with American entry into the war.

Vachon's striking images of buildings in the Upper Peninsula are a reminder of the degree to which he was influenced as a photographer by his mentor, Walker Evans: combining an uncompromising clean-edged realism with a subtle use of shadows and the clear light of a northern summer sky, the facades of homes, churches, mining structures, and storefronts become an indelible part of the landscape.

Aug. 1941, Trout Creek. Residents of a lumber town of the Upper Peninsula.
John Vachon. USF34-63536-D

Aug. 1941, Trout Creek. Old lumberjack. John Vachon. USF34-64025-D

Aug. 1941, Trout Creek. Logs at a lumber mill. John Vachon. USF34-63540-D

Aug. 1941, Laurium, a town in the copper range. Residents talking over a back fence.
John Vachon. USF34-63476-D

Aug. 1941, Franklin mine. A company-owned copper mining town on the copper range.
John Vachon. USF34-63474-D

Aug. 1941, Franklin mine. Copper mine. John Vachon. USF34-63478-D

Aug. 1941, Keweenaw County, a town in the copper range. An abandoned mining town. John Vachon. USF34-63543-D

Aug. 1941, Baraga. A church. John Vachon. USF34-63498-D

Aug. 1941, Ewen. Buildings. John Vachon. USF34-63510-D

Aug. 1941, Bruce's Crossing, a settlement of Finnish-Americans. Farm boy in a beer parlor on a Sunday afternoon. John Vachon. USF34-63542-D

II

Rural Lower Michigan, 1936–42

THE NUMBER OF PHOTOGRAPHS IN the FSA file for rural areas of the Lower Peninsula is small, with the exception of a thorough documentation of the fruit harvesting industry around the sandy dunes and fertile farmlands that stretch northward from the Indiana border along the coast of Lake Michigan. This is particularly surprising, because many of the rural and agricultural subjects the photographers documented in other states were readily available for study within the state of Michigan: diary farming, soil improvement and erosion control, grain cultivation, and the daily lives of families living on small Midwestern farms, struggling to survive economic hard times with the help of the Farm Security Administration's various programs. Although photographers created a rich record of these activities in Ohio and Indiana, Roy Stryker only infrequently sent them northward across the border into lower Michigan.

The FSA photographs of the Lower Peninsula's agricultural economy that do exist fall into three general groups: photographs recording Resettlement Administration work in the spring of 1936 near the beginning of that agency's efforts at land reclamation; John Vachon's elequent and thorough documentation (more than 250 photographs are in the file) of the growing, harvesting, and marketing of fruit in Benton Harbor and Berrien County in the summer of 1940 and of sugar beets in Saginaw in 1941; and Arthur Seigel's trips away from his native Detroit into the midlands of Michgan to record the wartime wheat harvest of 1942 and the tranquil rural landscapes and homescapes that came to symbolize for many Midwestern Americans the enduring values for which the war was being fought.

The reclaiming of overfarmed and deserted land for agricultural or forest productivity was central to the work of the Resettlement Administration, and agents directing such reclamation projects were among the RA field officers who requested that the "Historical Section" send photographers to document their sucesses. The Waterloo Land Use and the Allegan Reforestation projects illustrate the degree to which such rural improvements relied on manual labor using simple tools and thus also provided work for unemployed men during the depression. Work crews like those toiling to replant woodlands or prevent soil from blowing away were housed in camps and provided with meals and tools, giving photographers Paul Carter and Russell Lee an opportunity to provide a human dimension to their assignment to document landscape and erosion control techniques.

May 1936, Waterloo Land use project. Land being developed as a game preserve and recreational area by the U.S. Resettlement Administration. Game cover fence and food patch. Paul Carter. USF341-011084-B

May 1936, Waterloo land use project. The interior of a barn stacked with lumber.
Paul Carter. USF341-11097-B

May 1936, Allegan reforestation project of the U.S. Resettlement Administration. Wind erosion control. Branches are placed on the sand in the direction of the prevailing winds. Paul Carter. USF341-11071-B

June 1937, Allegan reforestation project of the U.S. Resettlement Administration. Chefs and their helpers in the camp kitchen. Russell Lee. USF34-30069-D

June 1937, Allegan reforestation project of the U.S. Resettlement Administration. A house in which people are still living on the project. Russell Lee. USF34-30062-D

July 1940, Milburg. Gas station attendant. John Vachon. USF34-61198-D

IN JUNE 1940 JOHN VACHON was sent to Michigan as part of a larger project, carried out in many parts of the country, to record the lives of migrant agricultural workers. In Benton Harbor he found an active market where fruit growers and distributors met to buy and sell, to gossip, and to shop. The town had long served as a country retreat for city dwellers fleeing the

July 1940, Benton Harbor. Gas station. John Vachon. USF33-1988-M5

summer heat of nearby Chicago. It was also home to a small new millennium religious sect called the "House of David," which Vachon mistakenly identified as an Orthodox Jewish community (note misinformation in his caption.) Benjamin Franklin Parnell, the self-proclaimed "King of the Israelite House of David," had founded the religious commune, which practiced traditional Christian communitarian life, at Benton Harbor in 1903. In 1940, members of the House of David operated a bakery and provided other services to vacationers.

July 1940, Benton Harbor. Rabbi in a synagogue at the House of David religious community. Jewish people come from Chicago and nearby large cities to spend summer vacations at the House of David. John Vachon. USF34-61197-D

July 1940, Benton Harbor. Fruit market. Growers pay 10 cents to drive a truck through the market; if produce is not sold at the end of the line it must enter through the gate again. John Vachon. USF34-61207-D

July 1940, Benton Harbor. Visitors at the fruit market. John Vachon. USF34-61083-D

THE AREA OF MICHIGAN JUST EAST of the long line of sand dunes that define the eastern shore of Lake Michigan has during much of the twentieth century been home to a bountiful fruit-growing industry. Strawberries, cherries, peaches, blueberries, and apples, each taking their turn in the harvesting season, were (and in many places still are) the mainstays of the economy from Benton Harbor in the south as far north as Traverse City and the Leelenau Peninsula. For the fruit growers, as for many who make their living from land held in families for generations, a successful harvest is an annual miracle: late frosts can destroy the fragile blossoms; insects and disease threaten the ripening fruit and require application of costly chemical sprays; sudden storms blowing off Lake Michigan can bruise and damage mature fruit ready for picking. Orchard keeping is year-round work; pruning and other tasks keep fruit growers and the region's permanent residents busy during winter months. The local labor supply has never been adequate for the summer harvest, however, and growers have depended on an annual influx of migrant labor to harvest the fragile fruit.

It was these seasonal laborers on whom John Vachon focused his camera lenses during the summer of 1940. Documenting the lives of migrant workers had been an important part of the work of the FSA during much of its existence. Dorothea Lange's images of migrants in the central valley of California in 1936 raised indignant protests from growers there, but were a powerful argument for the need for better housing, sanitation, and working conditions in the fields. Arthur Rothstein, writing to Roy Stryker from Florida in 1937, had urged a similar project to record the lives of eastern migrant farm workers, and based on his interviews with migrants outlined for Stryker the itinerary of those who followed the crops northward, ending in Michigan in the late summer. Not until 1940 did Stryker follow up on this suggestion.

The assignment fell to Rothstein's friend and protégé, John Vachon. In Berrien County, the tired faces of adults and children working in the strawberry fields and cherry orchards inspired Vachon to create a compassionate and intimate record of their daily lives. From the interiors of the small and overcrowded shacks provided by the growers, where a solemn girl posed in the act of setting the table or two shy sisters primped for an evening outing, to the busy processing plants where women in caps and aprons sorted rapidly through ripe cherries on their way to the canner, Vachon captured the humanity of this often-forgotten workforce.

That workforce included blacks as well as whites; the cheerful, self-contained young African-American cherry pickers and the anxious man seated on a porch (whom Vachon identified in another photograph as being sick) were part of a migrant stream of southern agricultural workers who might work adjacent to each other in the fields, but who occupied segregated bunkhouses and shacks.

July 1940, Berrien County. Michigan fruit grower and his two sons.
John Vachon. USF34-61135-D

THE FRUIT HARVESTERS OF BERRIEN COUNTY in 1940 were natives of the American South, black and white. The men, women, and children who worked in the demanding sugar beet fields of central Michigan were more likely to be immigrant or migrant Mexicans. In the years

July 1940, Berrien County. Wife and daughter of fruit farmer.
John Vachon. USF33-1987-M4

since the Second World War, the workforce of Michigan fruit pickers has become increasingly Hispanic; in some fruit-growing areas of the state, small settlements of Spanish-speaking former migrants have formed permanent communities. Arthur Siegel's series of photographs

July 1940, Berrien County. A nursery school for children of migratory workers run by the Women's Council for Home Missions. John Vachon. USF34-61082-D

documenting the Saginaw sugar beet workers is characteristic of much of the FSA treatment of people whom the majority culture had often dismissed: he took care to portray the family he chose as his subjects sympathetically, capturing the pride and dignity of young and old alike.

July 1940, Berrien County. Migrant strawberry picker. John Vachon. USF33-1975-M1

July 1940, Berrien County. Migrant father and daughter picking cherries.
John Vachon. USF33-1982-M3

July 1940, Berrien County. Migrant fruit workers. The cherries were picked for their own use. John Vachon. USF34-61121-D

July 1940, Berrien County. One of nine cabins adjoining the fruit packing plant. Families of 7 and 8 sometimes live in these $1.75 a week cabins. John Vachon. USF34-61159-D

July 1940, Berrien County. Daughter of a migrant fruit worker in a one-room cabin which rents for $1.75 a week. John Vachon. USF34-61169-D

July 1940, Berrien County. Migrant children. John Vachon. USF33-1973-M3

July 1940, Berrien County. Migrant girl fixing her sister's hair in a roadside camp of fruit workers. John Vachon. USF34-61209-D

July 1940, Berrien County. Migrant women at work in a packing plant.
John Vachon. USF34-61179-D

July 1940, Berrien County. Migrant fruit workers from Louisiana fixing a flat tire along the road. John Vachon. USF34-61118-D

July 1940, Berrien County. Cherry pickers. John Vachon. USF34-61176-D

July 1940, Berrien County. Migrant fruit worker. [The caption of another photograph of this worker identifies him as being sick.] John Vachon. USF34-61125-D

July 1940, Berrien County. Old barn used as a bunkhouse for migrant fruit pickers from the South. This grower employs only unmarried Negroes. John Vachon. USF34-61162-D

Aug. 1941, Saginaw County. Family of Mexican sugar beet workers.
John Vachon. USF34-63888-D

Fall 1941, Jackson. Soldier, who was granted a furlough to help with the harvesting on this farm, and farmer watching the threshing. Arthur Siegel. USW3-16414-E

WARTIME PRODUCTIVITY IN MICHIGAN IS often associated with the great industrial effort made in its cities—Detroit, Pontiac, Flint, and Saginaw. Yet, for much of the rural Lower Peninsula, the war effort also meant increasing the grain, dairy, and livestock yields that provided food for soldiers and civilian workers alike. So important was this work that soldier sons of farmers could be granted a furlough to bring in the crop during harvesttime.

Fall 194[1], Jackson. Threshing machine, truck carrying wheat, and straw wagons.
Arthur Siegel. USW3-16561-C

Fall 1941, Jackson. Wheat pouring out of the threshing machine.
Arthur Siegel. USW3-16439-E

July 1942, Birmingham (vicinity). Old style jewel stove and earthenware pots in a country home. Arthur Siegel. USF34-110005-C

July 1942, Birmingham (vicinity). Kitchen in a country house.
Arthur Siegel. USF34-110004-C

III

Industrial Michigan,
1939–41

1939, Detroit. Norman Bel Geddes and Nash-Kelvinator corporation officials inspecting a marked up model of new car. Arthur Siegel. USW3-16020-C

THE PHOTOGRAPHERS OF THE FARM SECURITY ADMINISTRATION, as the name of the agency suggests, were oriented more toward agricultural than toward industrial activities during the depression years. While Stryker did encourage his photographers to create a record of the small towns that served as commercial centers for agricultural regions, or of the urban processing of farm products, only rarely before 1940 did the agency examine heavy industry, urban problems, or industrial laborers.

Jan.–Feb. 1937, Flint. Strikers guarding a window entrance to the Fisher body plant, Factory no. 3. Sheldon Dick. USF34-40028-D

ONE EXCEPTION TO THIS GENERALIZATION is the brief photographic record, found in the FSA files and consisting of fifteen images, of the United Auto Workers sit-down strike in the Flint, Michigan, General Motors Fisher Body Plant in January and February 1937. The strike itself has become hallowed in the folklore of organized labor. For more than a month, a radical core of strikers battled local police and General Motors security forces. After a particularly violent confrontation in mid-January, the newly elected Democratic governor, Frank Murphy, sent National Guard troops to Flint, "not as strikebreakers, but as a buffer between the

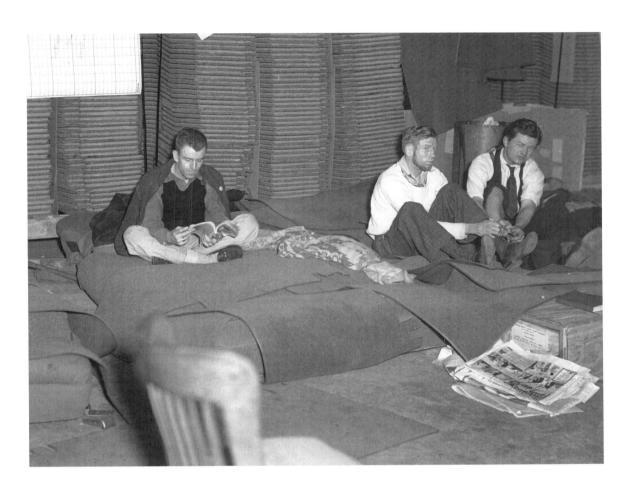

Jan.–Feb. 1937, Flint. The sleeping quarters for striking automobile workers in the Fisher body plant, Factory no. 3. Sheldon Dick. USF34-40029-D

contending forces."[2] In the end, General Motors agreed to bargain with the union leadership on a multi-plant agreement rather than insisting on dealing with local leaders on a plant by plant basis.

The photographer who captured these momentous events on film for the FSA/OWI

<hr />

2. Nelson Lichtenstein, *The Most Dangerous Man in Detroit: Walter Reuther and the Fate of American Labor* (New York: Basic Books, 1995), 77.

Jan.–Feb. [1937], Flint. The wives and sweethearts of the striking automobile workers, who are members of the ladies' auxiliary. Sheldon Dick. USF34-40025-D

file was Sheldon Dick, himself the reform-minded son of a Chicago industrialist. It is not clear whether Dick was a free agent when he photographed the strikers guarding the plant windows, relaxing on the automobile seats arranged into impromptu sleeping quarters, and being fed by the ladies' auxiliary, and later sold the prints to the FSA or OWI, or whether Roy Stryker

Jan.–Feb. [1937], Flint. National guardsmen with machine gun overlooking Chevrolet plants, factories no. 9 and no. 4, during a strike. Sheldon Dick. USF34-40023-D

hired him as a freelance photographer at the time. One of the photographs, of an exhausted striker sleeping in the Fisher Body Plant, Factory No. 3, brought him national recognition with its publication in the 1937 issue of the annual *U.S. Camera.*

Apr. 1939, Detroit. Meeting of the Michigan branch of the Communist party showing signs. Arthur Siegel. USW3-16470-C

FOR ORGANIZED LABOR AS A whole, and for unions in the Michigan auto industry in particular, the later years of the depression were crucial: the series of strikes begun by the successful UAW actions in Flint and elsewhere in Michigan led eventually to the emergence of a powerful new national union, the Congress of Industrial Organization, in which the United Auto Workers played a leading role. Radical organizers and supporters of the 1937 strikes included some members of the Socialist Party and the American Communist Party, and both of these organizations took a keen interest in their outcome, endorsing strikers' goals and tactics. Though a later generation, as well as many contemporary business and conservative political leaders, would condemn such Communist associations, during the late 1930s a number of workers supported the Communist Party as a political alternative to the mainline two-party political system.

June 1941, Dearborn. National Labor Relations Board election for union representation at
the River Rouge Ford plant. Workers balloting. Arthur Siegel. USW3-16337-C

THE PHOTOGRAPHS TAKEN BY ARTHUR SIEGEL four years after the Flint sit-down strikes
document quite a different, though equally significant, labor scene—the National Labor
Relations Board's supervision of a union election at the Ford plant in River Rouge. Siegel
probably completed them as a freelance photographer rather than under an FSA staff

June 1941, Dearborn. National Labor Relations Board election for union representation at the River Rouge Ford plant. NLRB official. Arthur Siegel. USW3-16325-E

assignment. They illustrate the pre-war culmination of UAW and CIO successes: the capitulation of the Ford Motor Company in April 1941 after a successful strike at the River Rouge plant. Strikers returned to work only after Ford agreed to negotiate with the UAW and abide by the results of an election supervised by the NLRB. Membership in Ford Local 600 of the UAW/CIO soared, including an influx into the union of black workers, who made up nearly one-sixth of the River Rouge plant's employees.[3]

3. Lichtenstein, *Most Dangerous Man*, 178–79; August Meier and Elliott Rudwick, *Black Detroit and the Rise of the UAW* (New York: Oxford University Press, 1979), 82–107.

Dec. 1939, Royal Oak. Father Coughlin's Shrine of the Little Flower.
Arthur Siegel. USW3-16743-C

FOR MANY WHO LIVED IN Michigan's industrial heartland, the chaos and violence of the strikes were both alarming and threatening. New Deal programs designed to deal with the underlying economic problems that helped generate the strikes were not embraced by all Americans, and in Royal Oak, Michigan, Rev. Charles Coughlin, the "Radio Priest," emerged in the mid-1930s as an important critic of President Franklin D. Roosevelt's economic policies. In the pre-war years, Royal Oak, where Father Coughlin presided over his Catholic parish at the Shrine of the Little Flower, was a northern suburb of Detroit whose tree-lined streets provided working- and middle-class families a safe haven from urban problems.

Dec. 1939, Royal Oak. A family listening to the radio and reading Father Coughlin's newspaper "Social Justice." Arthur Siegel. USW3-16733-C

For most Detroit residents, however, urban living provided amenities, not problems. In the summer before American entry into the Second World War, Arthur Siegel carried out an assignment to document the activities and services at one of Detroit's premier commercial establishments, the Crowley-Milner Department Store. He also visited a neighborhood beer

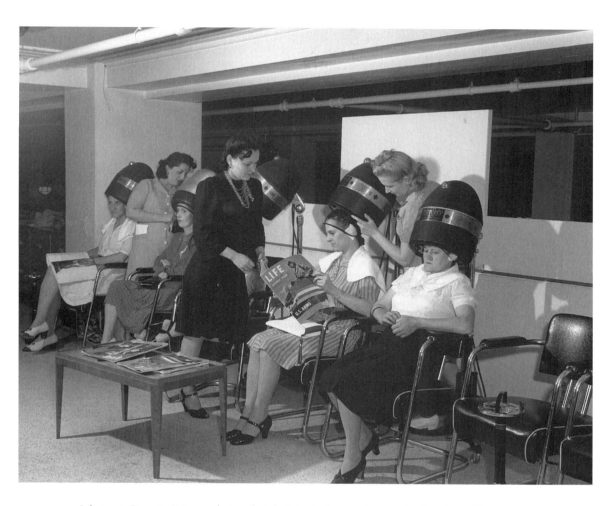

July 1941, Detroit. Women drying their hair in the beauty shop at the Crowley-Milner department store. Arthur Siegel. USW3-16623-C

parlor where German-Americans congregated after work. The woman reading *Life* magazine in the store's beauty salon provides an illuminating insight into the rapid public acceptance of a documentary photographic tradition in which she herself was tacitly participating as a subject.

Aug. 1941, Detroit (vicinity). Beer parlor. John Vachon. USF34-63674-D

IV

The Industrial Southeast
Prepares for War,
1941–42

1941, Detroit. Speakers' platform in front of a list of products manufactured by the automobile industry. Ernest Kanzler speaking at an early meeting of the Automotive Council for War Production. Arthur Siegel. USW3-16059-C

LONG BEFORE THE JAPANESE ATTACK on Pearl Harbor in the early morning hours of December 7, 1941, brought the United States in the Second World War as a full military participant, American industry played an important part in the growing European and Pacific conflicts. Despite strong pockets of isolationist sentiment against any American participation in the European conflict that began in 1939, President Roosevelt was determined not to be caught as unprepared as the nation had been in the First World War. Early in 1940 he began

1941, Detroit. Charles Wilson of the General Motors Corporation with a Navy man and an unknown manufacturer at an early meeting of the Automotive Council for War Production. Arthur Siegel. USW3-16058-C

enrolling leaders of American industry in systematic planning for the coming war effort. For Michigan, whose dominance in the ground transportation industry guaranteed that it would play a major role in wartime production, such planning was crucial to its transition from a peacetime to a wartime economy. The Automotive Council for War Production was an important agent of that planning. The 1941 list of products manufactured in Michigan or by Michigan-based companies associated with the automobile industry suggests how wide an impact the war would eventually have on the state.

Aug. 1941, Detroit (vicinity). Hudson Ordnance Plant from the backyard of a truck farm.
John Vachon. USF34-63716-D

BY THE SUMMER OF 1941, "Lend-Lease" had created a commitment to making America "the arsenal of democracy." The need for vehicles to be used in the Allied war efforts in Europe and Africa and in the buildup of military training in the United States had created an insatiable demand for Michigan's automotive and other heavy industrial products. The result was a boom in plant building, and a major housing crisis for the industrial workers recruited for the new manufacturing centers. Overnight, rural fields were replaced by ordnance and aircraft plants covering acres of ground. Nearby farmlands were snapped up by entrepreneurial real estate developers, and half-finished houses and trailer camps replaced farm buildings in the landscape.

Aug. 1941, Detroit (vicinity). Real estate office near tank plant refers to the Hudson Ordnance Plant. John Vachon. USF34-63715-D

Aug. 1941, Detroit (vicinity). House foundation which will be occupied by a defense worker and his family until spring, when he will complete the building.
John Vachon. USF34-63744-D

Aug. 1941, Detroit (vicinity). Ladies' toilet in the Daniels Trailer Park where many defense workers live. John Vachon. USF34-63659-D

Aug. 1941, Ypsilanti (vicinity). Concrete runway which extends over a mile from the buildings at Ford Bomber Plant at Willow Run, seen from the front porch of a farm. John Vachon. USF34-63711-D

WAR PRODUCTION PREPARATION, with the demands it put on the available pool of labor and the strains it put on the housing market, further disrupted the already precarious race relations of pre-war Michigan. The "great migration" of rural African-American families out of the Carolinas, Mississippi, Alabama, Arkansas, Tennessee, and other southern states, begun during the late nineteenth century, had accelerated during the agricultural depression of the 1920s. From the 1880s onward, Detroit was an important mecca for blacks fleeing the poverty and oppression of the post-Reconstruction south. African-American communities in Detroit and in other Michigan urban centers prospered, developed a vibrant cultural life, and supported the emergence of an important black urban elite of lawyers, ministers, medical and social workers, educators, and businessmen and women. Ironically, as they did so these communities faced growing resentment from second-generation European immigrants whose parents had fled persecution in Europe and sought economic opportunity in the industrial Midwest. Although the rigid southern system of legal segregation known as "Jim Crow" was never established in Michigan, a complex set of economic and social practices ensured a nearly complete physical separation of the races in neighborhoods and communities. The restrictive covenants adopted by whites to enforce this segregation were upheld in the courts and supported by local police power until the Supreme Court declared them unconstitutional in 1948. As a result, Detroit remained one of the most completely segregated urban centers in the nation throughout the Second World War.

As wartime industrial development moved into the suburbs, and particularly when it brought white workers into the vicinity of long-established black neighborhoods, the attempt to perpetuate residential segregation led literally to walls of separation. Like many FSA photographers, John Vachon was a social reformer who found such actions unsupportable. His photographs of African-American defense workers and their children segregated behind an eight-foot-high, half-mile-long wall in Ferndale, a northern suburb of Detroit, captured their pride and dignity in the face of prejudice, and illustrated vividly why the wall became "a blatant affront to blacks, as well as a glaring symbol of white racism in a northern city." One black woman thus cut off to prevent "contamination" of a white subdivision had lived in her house for fourteen years; another family had been residents of the area for eighteen years. To African-Americans themselves, and to reformers like Vachon, the comparison to the ghettos of Hitler's Europe was clear.[4]

4. Joe T. Darden, Richard Child Hill, June Thomas, and Richard Thomas, *Detroit: Race and Uneven Development* (Philadelphia: Temple University Press, 1987), 113.

Aug. 1941, Ypsilanti (vicinity). Edgewater Park Trailer Camp near the Ford Bomber Plant at Willow Run. John Vachon. USF34-63748-D

141

Aug. 1941, Ypsilanti (vicinity). Son of Mr. Nichols, a defense worker from Cass City, Michigan, who lives in a trailer at Edgewater Park. Mr. Nichols works in the Ford Bomber Plant at Willow Run. John Vachon. USF34-63678-D

Aug. 1941, Detroit (vicinity). Defense workers who live in a Negro settlement. John Vachon. USF34-63712-D

Aug. 1941, Detroit (vicinity). Negro children standing in front of half-mile concrete wall. This wall was built in August 1941, to separate the Negro section from a white housing development going up on the other side. John Vachon. USF34-63679-D

AFRICAN-AMERICANS WERE AN IMPORTANT source of labor for the new industrial plants springing up in the suburbs of Detroit, Flint, and Ypsilanti, and the need for new housing for these and other workers was one of a number of factors that led to wartime race riots as black and white workers contended for scarce housing and other resources. Such racial conflicts gave the United States a bad image in parts of the world where wartime cooperation with non-European peoples was essential. During the brief time that Stryker's "Historical Section" was located in the Office of War Information, it was called upon to deal with this problem.

The first serious race riot in Detroit during the war years took place at the Soujourner Truth Homes in February 1942. The development was originally designed as a segregated public housing project to house black war workers, located just north of the Polish-American suburb of Hamtramck in an area where black-white relations had been relatively friendly. It was briefly considered for white occupancy after local white residents expressed fear of property devaluation, and finally in January 1942 designated as a black project. The announcement in early February that the first residents were preparing to take occupancy provoked a violent reaction: the Ku Klux Klan burned a cross outside the project, vans carrying black tenants' furniture were overturned, and when black youths from Detroit rallied to protect the trucks and tenants, local police arrested the blacks. In outrage, the N.A.A.C.P. and UAW. supported the black tenants, demanding police protection for their peaceful intent, and in April African-American defense workers began moving into the project in earnest.[5]

The Office of War Information conducted an investigation into the incident, and a series of more than sixty photographs originally taken by Arthur Siegel as a freelance photographer for *Life* became part of the FSA/OWI "Historical Section" files as a result. Several different themes, calling attention to the contradictions between American celebration of its democratic values and its treatment of hardworking African-American citizens, emerge in the series as a whole, from which the handful selected here are representative. White workers, and initially even some middle-class blacks living in the area before the Sojourner Truth Homes were built, had expressed fears that project tenants would be lower-class migrants. Nearly half of Siegel's photographs attempted to counter that perception. Focusing on a dignified, well-dressed man who "worked at the Ford factory but was unable to live in a decent place until Sojourner Truth homes were open," Siegel first documented the family's living conditions in one of Detroit's older black neighborhoods. Siegel labeled it a "slum area," and his photographs deliberately illustrated it as substandard and degrading to those who lived there. In image after image, a loving, well-dressed, attractive African-American family prepared and ate its meals, children washed their hands, father and mother played with their baby, and older

5. Meier and Rudwick, *Black Detroit*, 176–83.

children did embroidery or read, portraying middle-class behavior and values clung to under adverse conditions.

At the riot site itself, in contrast to the police actions on the site, Siegel photographed one of the few arrests of a white participant—a real estate agent—in the melee, rather than one of the more than two hundred arrests of black participants. Overall, his images of the riot sympathetically portray the new tenants of the Soujourner Truth homes as orderly, neatly dressed, attractive, patriotic workers, and the white rioters who opposed them as the disruptive force. In his photographs Siegel attempted to show white audiences that his black subjects embraced the same traditional middle-class values of cleanliness, family loyalty, and hard work that they did. Although later wartime photographs by Siegel included images of integrated public events, Detroit nevertheless continued to be disrupted by confrontations between its black and white citizens during the war, with another, more serious riot taking place in 1943.

Feb. 1942, Detroit. Typical Negro business district. Arthur Siegel. USW3-16675-E

Feb. 1942, Detroit. Looking towards downtown from the slum area in the early morning. These are conditions under which families originally lived before moving to the Sojourner Truth housing project. Arthur Siegel. USW3-16706-C

Feb. 1942, Detroit. Coming up the stairway to a Negro's home. These are conditions under which families originally lived before moving to the Sojourner Truth housing project. Arthur Siegel. USW3-16657-E

Feb. 1942, Detroit. Negro family at dinner. These are conditions under which families
originally lived before moving to the Sojourner Truth housing project.
Arthur Siegel. USW3-16695-C

Feb. 1942, Detroit. Riot at the Sojourner Truth homes, a new U.S. Federal housing project, caused by white neighbors' attempt to prevent Negro tenants from moving in. Sign with American flag: "We want white tenants in our white community," directly opposite the housing project. Arthur Siegel. USW3-16549-C

Feb. 1942, Detroit. Riot at the Sojourner Truth homes, a new U.S. Federal housing project, caused by white neighbors' attempt to prevent Negro tenants from moving in. Furniture vans under police convoy. Arthur Siegel. USW3-16273-C

Feb. 1942, Detroit. Riot at the Sojourner Truth homes, a new U.S. Federal housing project, caused by white neighbors' attempt to prevent Negro tenants from moving in. Arrested white real estate operator who had been inciting the riot. Arthur Siegel. USW3-16274-C

Feb. 1942, Detroit. Riot at the Sojourner Truth homes, a new U.S. Federal housing project, caused by white neighbors' attempt to prevent Negro tenants from moving in. First Negro family moving into Sojourner Truth home. Arthur Siegel. USW3-16264-E

Feb. 1942, Detroit. Typical Negro family at Sojourner Truth homes.
Arthur Siegel. USW3-16280-C

V

The Industrial Southeast
at War: Wartime Industry,
1941–43

THE FOCUS OF THE "Historical Section" as a whole shifted after 1941 from documentation of hardy rural people enduring and rising above economic depression to that of a nation of civilians determined to support the war effort. In part, this was a natural result of the practical and strategic shift of the Section, first toward contract work for wartime agencies, and then under the administrative umbrella of the Office of War Information. The part of the FSA/OWI photographic file that encompasses Michigan illustrates this change. More than half of the fifteen hundred Michigan images are of wartime industrial work, and a large proportion of these are the work of Arthur Siegel. A native of Detroit, Siegel was called upon again and again to document, step by step, the processes of industrial war production in his hometown. One-time forays into the state by veteran FSA/OWI staff photographers John Vachon and Arthur Rothstein supplement this record, and the result is a composite portrait of industrial Michigan at war that illustrates the wide range of personal and economic activities on the home front.

For many civilians, war work began with an intensive period of training, equipping them with a new set of skills for the different occupations now in demand in Michigan's expanding war plants. Women in particular were recruited into war work that often differed dramatically from their pre-war employment. At the same time, many women continued to hold such traditionally female jobs as office typists or light industrial pieceworkers. Although war work has often been associated with assembly-line production in heavy industry, many war workers, whether secretaries and accountants or plant foremen and office managers, made their contributions to the war effort while sitting behind desks.

Spring 1942, Detroit. The Briggs School for training women aluminum workers.
Arthur Siegel. USW3-16222-C

Aug. 1942, Detroit. Class in fundamentals of radio under the defense training program sponsored by the U.S. government at the University of Detroit. Most of the students are already employed in war plants. John Vachon. USW3-7055-D

Spring 1942, Detroit. Office workers at work at the Chrysler Corporation.
Arthur Siegel. USW3-16395-C

Aug. 1942, Detroit (vicinity). Chrysler Corporation Dodge truck plant. A determined and efficient patriot is this veteran war worker. He plays an important role in keeping army trucks rolling to the combat areas. Arthur Siegel. USW3-7169-E

Sept. 1942, Detroit. Officials of the United Automobile Workers. Left to right: Walter P. Reuther, vice-president; R. J. Thomas, president; Richard T. Frankensteen, vice-president; George Addes, secretary-treasurer. Arthur Rothstein. USW3-7404-D

IN MICHIGAN, AS IN MANY other parts of the industrial north where organized labor was unwilling to sacrifice the hard-won gains of the immediate pre-war years, wartime production planning required cooperation of labor unions and their leaders with plant owners and managers. Recognizing this, and fearing the impact of strikes that could cripple industrial productivity, President Roosevelt created two new agencies to distribute and control labor resources: the War Manpower Commission, to establish priorities for the use of human resources, and the War Labor Board, to ensure corporate and labor cooperation. Under the latter, union membership and collective bargaining were given federal protection, but working conditions, wages, and hours were regulated under federal guidelines. In practice, this

Apr. 1942, Detroit. Election of officers to the Ford Local 600, United Automobile Workers, Congress of Industrial Organizations. 80,000 River Rouge Ford plant workers voted. Arthur Siegel. USW3-16247-C

sometimes meant that the appeal to support the war effort put union leadership into the position of sacrificing hard-won labor principles, such as that of premium pay for overtime work. Nevertheless, overall union membership rolls grew dramatically. The leadership as well as the rank and file of the UAW/CIO supported the war effort, but continued to insist that workers, not just corporate executives, should benefit from wartime profits, a position reflected in the slogan "Victory through equality of sacrifice." Despite internal political struggles, the UAW emerged after the war even stronger than it had been when it won the battle to organize the Ford Motor Company in 1941.

1942, Detroit. Delegates at the United Automobile Workers' international convention.
Arthur Siegel. USW3-16138-C

Aug. 1942, Detroit (vicinity). Chrysler Corporation Dodge truck plant. This watchman keeps a sharp eye over plant and grounds. Arthur Siegel. USW3-7161-E

THE AUTOMOBILE INDUSTRY RAPIDLY SHIFTED gears, from answering civilian needs for personal transportation to providing the ground-level mobility essential for modern warfare. Working under tight security conditions, Detroit manufactured, packed, and shipped thousands of army trucks, jeeps, and ambulances to fronts in Africa, the Far East, and Europe, notwithstanding initial shortages in rubber for tires. Mobilization of the automobile industry was accompanied by an intensive propaganda campaign, reminding workers of their responsibility to "Work to Win."

Aug. 1942, Detroit (vicinity). Chrysler Corporation Dodge truck plant. These tires are for Dodge army trucks. Overhead conveyors quickly move them from receiving docks to their proper places along the vast production line. Arthur Siegel. USW3-7125-C

Aug. 1942, Detroit (vicinity). Chrysler Corporation Dodge truck plant. Hundreds of deft operations are required to assemble and finish the long lines of Dodge army truck bodies that move daily to final production lines. Arthur Siegel. USW3-7180-E

169

Aug. 1942, Detroit (vicinity). Chrysler Corporation Dodge truck plant. Some of the thousands of Dodge Army ambulances lined up for delivery to the Army. Arthur Siegel. USW3-7110-C

Aug. 1942, Detroit [vicinity]. Chrysler Corporation Dodge truck plant. "Bring on the trucks and let me get 'em packed and on their way to whack 'Japs,'" says this barrel-chested war worker of might and main in the big busy plant. Arthur Siegel. USW3-7201-C

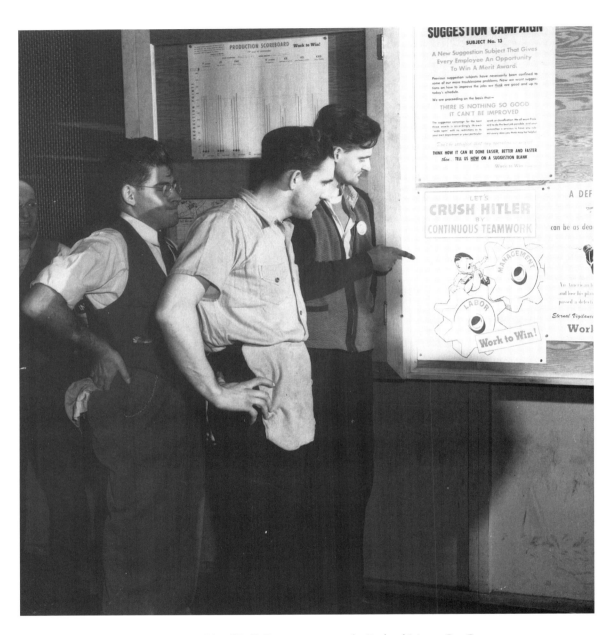

Jan. 1943, Detroit. Assembly of Rolls Royce engines at the Packard Motor Car Company.
Workmen inspecting a bulletin board. Arthur Siegel. USW3-12914-C

Nov. 1942, Detroit. Hanna furnaces of the Great Lakes Steel Corporation. General view of coke oven and quenching tower. Arthur Siegel. USW3-11195-C

ALTHOUGH THE AUTOMOTIVE INDUSTRY OFTEN seemed to dominate Michigan, other heavy industrial production also played a crucial role in the state's contributions to the war effort. Strategically located at a juncture of the Great Lakes where iron ore and coal could be efficiently transported for processing, Detroit was an important wartime center of steel production. Throughout the war, the coke ovens and blast furnaces of the Hanna division of the Great Lakes Steel Corporation lit up the Detroit River skyline. At Willow Run, and at the De Soto bomber plant, men and women assembled aircraft. At the Budd Wheel plant, a re-engineered assembly line turned out tens of thousands of 105mm shell casings. Working a War Labor Board standard forty-eight-hour week, and often putting in overtime hours, brought many employees a new prosperity.

Nov. 1942, Detroit. Hanna furnaces of the Great Lakes Steel Corporation. Coke being pushed from coke oven. Arthur Siegel. USW3-11209-C

Oct. 1942, Detroit. De Soto bomber plant. Nose section of B-26 bomber showing conveyor line running on the floor. Arthur Siegel. USW3-9467-C

Oct. 1942, Detroit. De Soto bomber plant. Final riveting operation on the life raft opening. Arthur Siegel. USW3-10183-C

Oct. 1942, Detroit. De Soto bomber plant. Women war workers wearing slacks check out at end of a shift. Arthur Siegel. USW3-9447-C

Jan. 1943, Detroit. Steps in the manufacture of casings for 105 mm. shells in the Budd wheel plant. Centering the shell forging. Beginning operation of machine work. Arthur Siegel. USW3-14281-C

Jan. 1943, Detroit. Steps in the manufacture of casings for 105 mm. shells in the Budd
wheel plant. Conveyor to the painting and packing department.
Arthur Siegel. USW3-14258-C

Jan. 1943, Detroit. Steps in the manufacture of casings for 105 mm. shells in the Budd wheel plant. Women inspecting shells before packing. Arthur Siegel. USW3-14261-C

May 1943, Detroit. Parke-Davis and Company, manufacturing chemists. Sterilizing medical solutions in autoclave. Arthur Siegel. USW3-33583-D

NOT ALL OF DETROIT'S WARTIME EFFORTS involved massive parts or preparation for mass destruction. Many war workers were engaged in providing other essential goods and services. At Parke-Davis and Company, Arthur Siegel carefully documented in more than 150 photographs the efforts of war workers manufacturing blood plasma units and other medical products needed at the front. At the Detroit River waterfront, land and water transport of wartime manufactured goods converged, as railroads brought cargoes to the loading docks for ferries and deep-water vessels. At the Wayne County Airport, a U.S. Army Air Corps air ferry command base readied bombers manufactured at plants in Detroit and Willow Run for

May 1943, Detroit. Parke-Davis and Company, manufacturing chemists. Final assembly and packaging of complete blood plasma units. Arthur Siegel. USW3-33613-D

Apr. 1943, Detroit. A trainyard with car ferries and loading docks.
Arthur Siegel. USW3-21645-C

Apr. 1943, Detroit. A Diesel engineer in the cab of a locomotive.
Arthur Siegel. USW3-21642-C

Oct. 1942, Detroit. Wayne County Air Port Ferry Command. Bombers.
Arthur Siegel. USW3-9472-C

Sept. 1942, Detroit. Wayne county airport, a U.S. Air Corps air ferry command base 16 miles from Detroit, Michigan. Sector status report. A mechanic is lifting a tool box. Arthur Siegel. USW3-8699-C

VI

Life on the Michigan Home Front, 1941–43

Aug. 1942, Detroit. City Hall. John Vachon. USW3-7060-D

THE YEARS OF THE WAR brought sacrifice and prosperity, a sense of common purpose, and a renewed energy to Michigan, reflected in the photographs that John Vachon, Arthur Siegel, and Arthur Rothstein took of its people for the Office of War Information. The streets and public buildings of wartime Detroit crackled with activity. From the baroque splendor of its Romanesque City Hall to the clean lines of the new Art Deco federal post office building; from the traffic-clogged downtown commercial streets and the bustling movement of Cadillac Square to quieter ethnic neighborhoods; in schools, churches, and universities—Michigan citizens went about their daily business, keeping a steady eye on the progress of the war, coping with consumer shortages and personal loss, raising their children, and hoping for a better future.

July 1942, Detroit. Exterior of the modern Federal Post Office building.
Arthur Siegel. USF34-110173-C

July 1942, Detroit. Looking down Griswold St. towards the Union Guardian building. Arthur Siegel. USF34-110159-C

Aug. 1942, Detroit. Cadillac Square. John Vachon. USW3-7077-D

Aug. 1942, Detroit. Polish district with St. Florian's Roman Catholic church in the background. John Vachon. USW3-7044-D

July 1942, Detroit. Looking southwest from the McAbee Building toward Wayne
University. Arthur Siegel. USF34-110031-C

Aug. 18, 1942, Detroit. Morning extra. John Vachon. USW3-7078-D

Aug. 1942, Detroit. Coast Guard recruiting station. John Vachon. USW3-7073-D

Spring 1942, Detroit. Waiting in line at sugar rationing board.
Arthur Siegel. USW3-16226-C

WHATEVER THEIR BUSINESS, MOST CIVILIANS spent much of the war waiting in line:
Waiting to receive ration coupons for such commodities as sugar, butter, coffee, meat, cheese,
shoes, tires, and gasoline, then waiting in line again to purchase these items;
Waiting for buses to take them home from work
Waiting for trains and buses to take them to more distant places.
Even mailboxes seemed to wait in line for the delivery of good or bad news.

July 1942, Detroit. People lined up waiting for a bus at 5 o'clock.
Arthur Siegel. USF34-110175-C

Aug. 1942, Detroit. Greyhound bus station. John Vachon. USW3-7102-D

Sept. 1942, Cass Lake, near Pontiac. Karl Axel Westerberg looking for mail in the rural free delivery mail box. He and his son, Eric, drive 25 miles a day to work in the Ford motor car company plant at Dearborn. Arthur Rothstein. USW3-7397-D

1942, Detroit. Ceremonies at the Hudson Naval Ordnance Plant on the occasion of the Navy "E" Award. Arthur Siegel. USW3-16093-E

SUPPORT FOR THE WAR EFFORT BECAME a patriotic duty, urged on by recruiting and war bond posters, and celebrated in public ceremonies. Encouragement to participate came in many forms. At the workplace, recognizing group effort by the ceremonial presentation of "E" awards for exceeding wartime production goals brought politicians and people together with expressions of commitment to common goals.

Sept. 1942, Detroit (vicinity). Ceremonies at the presentation of the Army and Navy E Award to the Briggs Manufacturing Company. Governor Patrick Van Wagoner of the state of Michigan. Arthur Siegel. USW3-9150-C

Sept. 1942, Detroit (vicinity). Ceremonies at the presentation of the Army and Navy E
Award to the Briggs Manufacturing Company. Worker who is a war veteran.
Arthur Siegel. USW3-9181-E

Fall 1942, Detroit. Scrap collected for salvage at a rally sponsored by the Work Projects
Administration at the State Fair Grounds. Arthur Siegel. USW3-16201-C

CREATING PUBLIC OPPORTUNITIES FOR ORDINARY citizens to contribute to these common
goals sometimes juxtaposed the solemn with the silly, and brought out unexpected creativity,
good humor, and cooperation. Arthur Siegel's coverage of a rally to promote the collection of
scrap metal for the war effort, sponsored by the WPA late in 1942, just before that agency was
disbanded, illustrates the zeal with which average Americans responded to such opportunities.
An integrated crowd gathered at the Michigan State Fair Grounds, passing piles of "Scrap for
the Jap," and savoring an evening of entertainment that brought together samples of a wide
range of ethnic cultural expression, reflecting the diversity of the Detroit community.

Fall 1942, Detroit. Audience at an entertainment at a scrap salvage rally sponsored by the Work Projects Administration at the State Fair Grounds. Arthur Siegel. USW3-16216-C

Fall 1942, Detroit. Church dignitaries at a scrap salvage rally sponsored by the Work Projects Administration at the State Fair Grounds. Arthur Siegel. USW3-16181-C

Fall 1942, Detroit. Entertainers performing at a scrap salvage rally sponsored by the Work Projects Administration at the State Fair Grounds. Arthur Siegel. USW3-16166-C

Fall 1942, Detroit. Entertainers performing at a scrap salvage rally sponsored by the Work Projects Administration at the State Fair Grounds. Arthur Siegel. USW3-16197-C

Aug. 1942, Detroit. Briggs Stadium. John Vachon. USW3-7071-D

POPULAR PRE-WAR FORMS OF ENTERTAINMENT continued during the war, although some activities were hampered by wartime restrictions and demands. The Detroit Tigers, like most professional baseball teams during the war, faced both loss of young players to the armed services and diminished crowds as fans worked long shifts and overtime that kept them away from Briggs stadium. Detroit's young women continued to primp and prepare for an evening out or a stroll in the park with a special soldier or sailor, but the exodus of great numbers of men into the armed services meant a shortage of available males. The absence of male partners

Aug. 1942, Detroit. Detroit vs. Cleveland ball game at Briggs Stadium.
John Vachon. USW3-7094-D

for social events and the increase for these young women of disposable income from their war production employment created a ready audience for the styling and fashion shows (often sponsored by the companies for whom they worked) which hundreds of young women attended.

Summer 1941, Detroit. Girl putting on lipstick and another girl straightening seams in her stocking. Arthur Siegel. USW3-15993-C

July 1942, Detroit. Sailors and girls at zoological park. Arthur Siegel. USF34-110135-E

Dec. 1941, Detroit. Winners at a hair styling show. Arthur Siegel. USW3-16409-C

Spring 1942, Detroit. Two Chrysler girl workers at Saks Fifth Avenue store following a
fashion show presented by the Chrysler Girls' Club of the Chrysler Corporation.
Arthur Siegel. USW3-16365-C

THE CHILDREN OF MICHIGAN PORTRAYED in the images throughout this book participated in much of the activity of wartime civilian life: attending rallies and watching parades, waiting in lines or in bus stations, competing in scrap metal drives, helping their parents with victory gardens. They were more fortunate than many whose childhood was shadowed by the war, including the children of London, who experienced the Blitz or who were separated from their parents when sent for safety into the countryside or overseas, and the Jewish children of Europe or the Japanese-American children of the Pacific coast, who were compelled with their parents to give up their homes and were sent to concentration or relocation camps. The FSA/OWI photographers in Michigan, as elsewhere, seemed to take a particular pleasure in focusing their camera lenses on the faces and ordinary activities of children. Perhaps because children were less self-conscious in the photographer's intruding presence, perhaps because the photographers found in their exuberance and playfulness a respite from the grimness of wartime headlines or casualty reports, the portraits of children they created are among the most memorable images of the FSA/OWI file, a great legacy to those now-grown children and to their children and grandchildren.

Despite wartime restrictions on nonessential long-distance travel, one of Michigan's great institutions for young people and the arts continued to operate during the war. The National Music Camp at Interlochen was founded in 1927 by conductor Dr. Joseph E. Maddy and his friend, the composer Howard Hanson, and has provided training in classical music to children and youth from Michigan, the region, the nation, and around the world for more than seventy years. Arthur Siegel escaped from the heat of Detroit late in the summer of 1942 on an assignment to document the activities of Maddy's young musicians. His more than ninety Interlochen photographs in the file affirm the continuity of the arts during war and peace alike. Generations of young French horn players have posed in the diagonal line of shining brass and concentrated faces in an image that has become symbolic of Interlochen. The timelessness of the invitation to swimmers of the cool waters of Lakes Wapakanetta and Wappakeness, of young players performing the work of the great masters, of great teachers passing on to the next generation their skills and knowledge, make Siegel's Interlochen photographs a fitting conclusion for this essay on children in wartime Michigan.

July 1942, Detroit. Middle-class boys and girls. Arthur Siegel. USF34-110043-C

July 1942, Detroit. Group of bicyclists. Arthur Siegel. USF34-110002-C

217

July 1942, Detroit. Little girl with ice cream cone in the zoological park.
Arthur Siegel. USF34-110117-E

Aug. 1942, Interlochen. National music camp where 300 or more young musicians study symphonic music for 8 weeks each summer. French horns during symphony practice. Arthur Siegel. USW3-6803-C

Aug. 1942, Interlochen. National music camp where 300 or more young musicians study symphonic music for 8 weeks each summer. Swimming dock. Arthur Siegel. USW3-6769-E

Aug. 1942, Interlochen. National music camp where 300 or more young musicians study symphonic music for 8 weeks each summer. Dr. Maddy, director of the camp, conducts the symphony orchestra. Arthur Siegel. USW3-6796-C

Aug. 1942, Interlochen. National music camp where 300 or more young musicians study symphonic music for 8 weeks each summer. Percy Grainger, famous pianist and composer, with a student. Arthur Siegel. USW3-6792-C

July 1943. Detroit (vicinity). A hayfield. Arthur Siegel. USW3-35827-D

THE FSA/OWI PHOTOGRAPHERS SOMETIMES REFERRED to tranquil landscapes that evoked nostalgia for a rural past and invoked pride in the beauty of America as "FSA Cheesecake" shots. Though they occasionally disparaged such work, they did it superbly. Arthur Siegel was a product of the urban streets of Detroit, but in July 1943, not far from the city, he captured an image of a quintessential rural Michigan landscape that reminds us all of the importance of place to the people who have lived, worked, and played in its embrace.

THE
PHOTOGRAPHERS

Russell Lee (1903–86)

The first photographers from the Farm Security Administration project to come to Michigan were Russell Lee and Paul Carter. Russell Lee became one of the best known and most prolific of the FSA photographers, working for Stryker longer than any of the others. He joined the "Historical Section" in the fall of 1936 and moved with it and Stryker to the Office of War Information in 1942, leaving in 1943 to become a photographer for the US Army Air Transport Command. Photographic historian Hank O'Neal, in *A Vision Shared*, called Lee "the ideal FSA photographer," because he brought to his work with cameras and film a background as a chemist and as an artist. Born in Ottawa, Illinois, in 1903, Lee attended Culver Military Academy in Indiana, graduated from Lehigh University with a degree in chemical engineering in 1925, and worked as a chemist for a manufacturer of roofing materials. In 1929 he quit his job as a plant manager in Kansas City to attend the California School of Fine Arts, and in the depths of the depression he joined an art community in Woodstock, New York, with his first wife, Doris.

Lee soon became part of the innovative circle studying at the Art Students League in New York City. In 1935 he bought his first camera, a Contax, intending to use it as an aid to improve his drawing. Instead, at the age of thirty-two, he realized he was a photographer. When the FSA organized a photographic exhibition in New York in 1936, Lee admired it, determined that documentary photography was what he wanted to do, and went to Washington, D.C., where he persuaded his friend, artist and photographer Ben Shahn, to introduce him to Roy Stryker. Although the FSA had no openings for a photographer in the spring of 1936, Stryker was impressed with the photographs Lee showed him, a series of images published in *Colliers* magazine documenting bootleg coal miners in Pennsylvania.

225

The opportunity came in September, when Carl Mydans resigned from the FSA to go to work for the new *Life* magazine. Stryker hired Lee at a salary of $2,600 a year, and sent him out on the road in mid-October for "two immediate jobs" documenting FSA projects in New Jersey. By the time he had finished that road trip in July 1937 Russell Lee had traveled to Ames, Iowa, to photograph tenant farmers; up and down the Mississippi River, recording the great flood of the winter of 1936–37; and back east to an Indiana farm to document the daily life of a hired man. During April and May, Stryker sent Lee up into the "cut-over" district of the upper Midwest: Minnesota, Wisconsin, and Michigan's Upper Peninsula.

Russell Lee never photographed for the FSA in Michigan again, but the people he met in the Upper Peninsula and the conditions they faced were indelibly etched in his mind. After 1937, most of his work for the "Section" was in the West. He and his second wife, Jean, pioneered in documenting America's small towns, and in Chicago Lee created one of the few systematic and sympathetic depression-era photographic documentary records of African-American life in the ghettos of a northern city. More than any of the other FSA photographers, he was always conscious of "shooting for the file." "You never really tried to break it down to build a story," he insisted; "it was still raw material there in the files for someone else to edit from, . . . just a great mass of raw material." The America he saw in his travels was down, but not out. His wife, Jean, described the "tremendous pride" of the people they met everywhere: "They were living on the ditchbanks, they were picking wild berries to eat, because there was nothing else. But it was very seldom that you found a person who really felt whipped. Somehow they were going to go on until this afternoon, at least. Now they didn't know what was going to happen tomorrow, but until late this afternoon, somehow it would work out all right."

After the war, Russell Lee continued briefly in government service, as a photographer for the Coal Mines Administration of the Interior Department in 1946–47. Thereafter he combined industrial, magazine, and freelance photography with teaching, first from 1948 to 1965 at the University of Missouri Photo Workshop, where he eventually became director. In spring 1951 he again worked for Stryker, contributing several hundred images to the Pittsburgh Photographic Library documentary project. From 1965 until his death in 1986 he taught at the University of Texas, Department of Fine Arts.

Sources: *Hank O'Neal, A Vision Shared: A Classic Portrait of America and Its People, 1935–1943* (New York: St. Martin's Press, 1976); Martin Marix Evans, ed., *Contemporary Photographers*, 3d ed. (New York, 1995), 640–41; Archives of American Art, Smithsonian Institution, oral history interview with Russell and Jean Lee, oral history interview with Roy Stryker; correspondence, Roy Stryker Papers, Photographic Archives, University of Louisville, microfilm edition. Quotation is from p. 30 of oral history interview with Russell and Jean Lee.

Paul Carter (1903–38)

In direct contrast to Russell Lee, Paul Carter is one of the least known of the photographers whom Roy Stryker hired to participate in the work of the Farm Security Administration. Born in 1903, the fifth of seven children of the Reverend John Franklin Carter, rector of St. John's Church in Williamstown, Massachusetts, Paul lived in the shadow of his accomplished older brother, John Franklin Carter Jr. All six of the Carter boys went to Yale, but unlike his older brothers, Paul dropped out. In his memoir of the family's growing up days, John, who wrote a syndicated column under the name "Jay Franklin" for the *Washington Post*, casually remarked that "Paul became a professional photographer, with one interlude as a cowboy in British Columbia."

Indeed, it was through the influence of this older brother, an intimate of President Franklin D. Roosevelt who served as an undersecretary of Agriculture between 1934 and 1936, that Paul Carter came to work for the FSA in the first place. In March 1936, "Jay Franklin" was appointed to the Resettlement Administration as a special research assistant to Rexford Tugwell, becoming the agency's director of information, to whom Roy Stryker reported. Stryker remembered Jay Franklin Carter as one of the few administrators for whom he had any respect—largely because he let Stryker run his photographic "History Section" without interference, and put Stryker in charge of all of the photographic work of the agency as a whole.

From the beginning, staff later remembered, Paul Carter suffered from the knowledge that his was a political appointment; he seemed to the secretaries not to enter into the esprit de corps of the agency. "I never did think Paul Carter was too happy," Charlotte Aiken confided when interviewed by Richard Doud for the Archives of American Art oral history project. Laughing at the memory, she added that his letters claiming reimbursement for travel were "really something. . . . He'd take a slim view of statistics and speedometer readings, and he said, 'Oh, you figure that out.'" Stryker remembered him as overweight, sick with the disease from which he eventually died, unhappy about traveling, and not a very good photographer.

Carter's work with the RA/FSA in 1936–37 was brief: in May 1936, working with Russell Lee, Carter shot a series of photographs of the Allegan reforestation project and a similar "Waterloo Land Use" project in southwestern Michigan. After photographing in Minnesota and Michigan in the spring of 1936, he made trips to document the construction of several RA "Homesteads" projects in North Dakota, Iowa, Michigan, Minnesota, Indiana, and Virginia and completed a brief assignment in New England. When he left the FSA in 1937, he went to work in a camera shop in Hanover, New Hampshire, near the campus of Dartmouth. He died in Hanover on July 20, 1938, of a pulmonary hemorrhage.

Sources: Archives of American Art, Smithsonian Institution, oral history interviews with Roy Stryker, Charlotte Aiken, and Arthur Rothstein; John Franklin Carter, *The Rectory Family* (New York: Coward-McCann, 1937); obituary, *Hanover Gazette*, July 28, 1938.

Sheldon Dick (1906–50)

Like Paul Carter, Sheldon Dick was one of the lesser-known photographers of the Farm Security Administration. Born in 1906 in Lake Forest, Illinois, as the younger son of the "mimeograph king," A. B. Dick, Sheldon Dick seems on the surface an odd candidate for inclusion within the documentary photographic ranks of the FSA. Wealthy and privileged, he attended Cambridge University and became a prominent socialite with reform sympathies who attempted with mixed success to find a useful role for himself in depression-era America. He had some experience as a photographer, having provided the illustrations for a travel book, *Mexican Journey* (1936), he coauthored with Edith Mackie. The book was reviewed critically by the *New York Times*, which noted that "The group of photographs adds little to the value of the volume."

Stryker met Sheldon Dick through publishers Henry Lester and Willard Morgan. On one of his trips to New York, they asked Stryker if he would "take Sheldon down to Washington on more or less a dollar a year." Stryker sent him out with a shooting script to photograph out-of-work miners in a Shenandoah hard coal town, "a fantastic little town and you could [have] practically set your cameras up and triggered them and have them on rotate and gotten pictures," but he judged Dick's results as "lousy, just plain lousy." Despite this assessment, Stryker kept the young photographer and his minimal payroll on at FSA, though only briefly. During 1937 and 1938, Dick was assigned to cover hurricane damage in New England and FSA clients in Pennsylvania and Maryland. Years later Stryker remembered him sympathetically as a "terribly nice boy" who realized only too well that he was "a checkbook for the left-wingers of the time." He later used his wealth to do a movie on zinc mining. Tragically, in the spring of 1950 he killed himself and his third wife in their suburban New York home. The 1939 photograph published in the news stories recording his death shows a serious, slightly built man firmly holding a Speed Graphic camera, pensively eyeing the unseen camera taking his portrait.

Sheldon Dick's photographs of the Shenandoah hard coal miners may have seemed "lousy" to Stryker, but the series of photographs he shot inside the General Motors Fisher Body plant in Flint, Michigan, when a sit-down strike immobilized the auto industry in January 1937, are memorable. The strike itself is legendary in the annals of twentieth-century labor activism. For weeks the men occupied the plant in order to dramatize their demands for better wages and working conditions, and for union recognition. Only sympathetic observers were allowed into the plant to report on the strikers' plight and purpose. Dick's photographs of the strikers climbing ladders to bring supplies into the second-story window of the barricaded plant; of the wives and sweethearts in the "women's auxiliary" who prepared food for their men; and of the National Guard, with their artillery gathered outside the plant, brought the drama of the strike to the nation. His image of striking workers bedding down to sleep on the upholstered seats of the automobiles they were refusing to assemble was published in the 1937 US Camera annual as one of the best photographs of the year.

Sources: Archives of American Art, Smithsonian Institution, oral history interview with Roy Stryker; Sheldon Dick and Edith Mackie, *Mexican Journey: An Intimate Guide to Mexico* (New York: Dodge Publishing Company, 1936); *New York Times*, September 27, 1936, and May 13, 1950, p. 34; on the strike, see Nelson Lichtenstein, *The Most Dangerous Man in Detroit: Walter Reuther and the Fate of American Labor* (New York: Basic Books, 1995).

Arthur Siegel (1913–78)

Of the more than 1,500 photographs of Michigan in the files of the Farm Security Administration and Office of War Information housed at the Library of Congress, nearly half were taken by Detroit-born photographer Arthur Siegel. Yet, as prolific as he was, Siegel's name is much less frequently associated with FSA/OWI than with his later work as an innovative photographic artist in the 1950s and 1960s, pushing the limits of 35 mm color film. Born in Detroit and educated in its public schools and at the University of Michigan and Wayne State University, Siegel first began photographing seriously in 1927, while only a teenager. In 1937–38 Laszlo Moholy-Nagy offered Siegel a scholarship to his New Bauhaus School in Chicago, an institution which became the prestigious Chicago Institute of Design. Later Siegel himself became a member of the Institute faculty, working there from 1946 until 1978 and ending his career as chair of its Photography Department and one of its most respected teachers.

Siegel began his professional photographic and teaching careers in Detroit in the 1930s. Todd Webb, a young photographer who later worked for Roy Stryker on the Standard Oil of New Jersey project, remembered that when he joined the Chrysler Camera Club in 1938, Siegel was a leader and a photography teacher in Detroit. He taught photography at Wayne University and worked in the Visual Education Department of the Detroit Public Schools. In another educational venture, Siegel brought the then relatively unknown Ansel Adams to Detroit in 1941 to do a photography workshop at the Chrysler Club. Between 1935 and 1942, Siegel worked extensively in Detroit as a commercial freelance photographer who specialized in industrial and documentary photography even as he was developing his experimental techniques in color photography and the photogram.

Michigan was Siegel's home state, and Detroit his backyard. Probably Siegel worked for Stryker much of the time on a freelance basis, hired for a project rather than on salary. During 1941 and 1942, he painstakingly documented for the OWI the assembly-line details of wartime Detroit, including the manufacture of essential blood plasma units and pain medication at the Parke-Davis and Company pharmaceutical plant; the training of women war-workers at the Briggs school; the manufacture of army vehicles at Chrysler plants; the operation of coke ovens and blast furnaces at the Hanna Steel Furnace; and the assembly of shell casings at the Budd Wheel Plant and of B-26 Bombers at the De Soto plant. In hundreds of file photographs, men and women stand erectly at their workstations, demonstrating step by step for the photographer the functioning of heavy machinery or the dexterity required for delicate wiring operations.

As Russell Lee had done in Chicago, Arthur Siegel carried out in Detroit one of the few urban photographic projects of the FSA/OWI to document the lives of inner-city African-Americans. The vibrant African-American community in Detroit became during the early years of the war an untapped labor pool for the rapidly expanding wartime industrial production of the region. Wartime production-line integration, however, led to housing and transportation problems for many blacks. In an important series of images recording the attempt to provide black and white workers alike with housing nearer the new war-production plants, Siegel documented both the conditions in an older black neighborhood near Detroit's downtown and the rioting by white workers who were attempting to prevent black families from moving into the Sojourner Truth homes built for them on the outskirts of Detroit.

In addition to photographing Michigan's largest city, Siegel also traveled into the nearby countryside during 1942 and 1943 to record the important work of bringing in the wheat harvest. He also escaped the city heat in the summer of 1942 to photograph the young musicians at Interlochen National Music Camp in activities and uniforms that remain almost unchanged more than fifty years later. Roy Stryker recognized Siegel as a fine photographer and a brilliant mind, but the two men never really got along. Stryker certainly never provided Siegel with one of his famous "shooting scripts," and only rarely hired him to do work outside of Michigan. The work he did in his home state, however, remains an important legacy of its wartime experiences.

Sources: *U.S. Camera Annual*, 1941; biographical entry by Larry Viskochil in Martin Marix Evans, ed., *Contemporary Photographers*, 3d ed. (New York: St. James Press, 1995), 1025–26; Robert Doty, ed., *Photography in America* (New York: Whitney Museum of Art, 1974); Archives of American Art, Smithsonian Institution, oral history interviews with Todd Webb, Harry M. Callahan, and Roy Stryker.

John Vachon (1914–75)

The final two FSA/OWI photographers who came to the state of Michigan, John Vachon and Arthur Rothstein, were good friends, and, like Russell Lee, worked under Stryker for nearly the entire duration of the "Historical Section." John Vachon began work at the agency almost by accident: a native of St. Paul, Minnesota, with an undergraduate degree in English, he came to Washington, D.C., in 1934 to do graduate work in Elizabethan poetry at Catholic University, but by the spring of 1936 was looking for any work he could find. Through his congressman he found out that the Resettlement Administration had an opening for an "assistant messenger" in the Historical Section of the Information Division. Roy Stryker hired him in part to carry messages, but mostly to copy captions from file cards onto the back of 8 x 10 photographs.

By his own admission knowing nothing about either photography or the Resettlement Administration, before long Vachon was turning over the photographs he labeled to look at them. Within a year he was promoted to the position of file clerk, and was asking Stryker if he could borrow a camera to take out on weekends. When Arthur Rothstein, Ben Shahn, and Walker Evans found out what he was doing, each went out of his way to give Vachon some basic instruction, and each in his own way taught the neophyte cameraman to see the world with new eyes. In particular, Evans's singular approach to documentary photography as an art form, one in which the photographer created a vital, demanding image by carefully observing and framing with his lens rather than forming with his hands or brush, had a permanent liberating influence on Vachon's development of a vision and a style all his own.

From 1937 until 1940, Vachon's official title was "Assistant Clerk," and the organizational system for photographs as it functioned within the agency during its working years was largely Vachon's creation. "I organized them on the basis that there were forty-eight states, so all pictures from Alabama went under 'Alabama,' with classifications under that which tended to keep what would be picture stories—things taken in the same town, or of the same family—together with a title," he remembered. Because the photographs were made available to users at no charge, there was an increasing demand for them. As the file clerk who located the requested images and filled the orders, Vachon probably came to know the "file" better than any of the photographers out in the field—perhaps even better than Stryker himself. "I was terribl[y] involved with the building up of the file," he mused nearly thirty years later. "Being with it all the time, I sort of fell in love with it." Vachon took that familiarity with the file into the field with him when Stryker began sending him on occasional extended photographic trips in 1938 and then promoted him to the official position of "Junior Photographer," at a salary of $150 a month, in 1940.

Vachon made more trips to Michigan for the FSA than any of the others for whom the state was not home, and saw a greater, more diverse cross section of the state than anyone except Siegel. In July 1940 he carried out the Michigan portion of a long-standing goal of Stryker's—to document the lives of permanent migrant farm laborers as they followed a regular seasonal harvesting route from Florida northward to Michigan. Sympathetic images of migrant workers were one of the trademarks of the FSA, one which frequently placed Stryker and his photographers in political hot water with growers, particularly in California, where the Resettlement Administration had played a major—and unpopular—role in building housing for agricultural workers. As early as January 1937, Arthur Rothstein had begun an investigation of the migrants of the East which he urged Stryker to let him develop more fully:

Many migrants have been following the same route for five years. I got a list of the places one of them has been to in the past year:

Belle Glade, Deerfield, Fla.	-Dec.& Jan.
Homestead, Fla.	-Jan.& Feb.
Plant City, Fla.	-Feb.
Stark, Fl.	-March
Pomelatoula, La.	-April
Bald Knob, Ark.	-May
Humboldt, Tenn.	-May
Padukah, Ky.	-May–June
Barada, South Haven, Riverside, Mich.	-June
Bear Lake, Hart, Shelby, Mich.	-July–Aug

In July 1940 it was John Vachon, rather than Rothstein, who caught up with those migrants as they picked and processed the fruit harvest of Barada, South Haven, and Berrien County, Michigan. His images capture both the weariness of the adults and the combination of toughness and wistfulness in the children living in the substandard housing and doing the backbreaking work that was their daily lives.

A year later Vachon was back in Michigan, this time with an entirely different assignment: retracing Russell Lee's steps into the cut-over district and the abandoned mining communities of the Upper Peninsula. In his photographs of the skeletal towers framing the low-lying houses of out-of-work copper miners, one can see the persistent influence of Walker Evans's stark frontal realistic photographic style. Vachon also photographed people whose obvious enjoyment of long August days softened the image of the economic hardship his captions described. Perhaps the bright economic reflections of wartime production were already reaching into the Upper Peninsula; as he drove south that August, Vachon documented the building boom, housing shortages, and real estate frenzy surrounding the construction of the new Hudson Ordnance Plant outside of Detroit.

On his third visit to Michigan, near the end of his final road trip for a "Historical Section" that was now part of the Office of War Information and about to go out of business, Vachon observed the wartime lives of Detroiters. As always, he "shot for the file," catching the patience and good humor of ordinary people waiting in lines to ride buses or see a parade. Shortly after photographing the Coast Guard recruiting station in Detroit's Cadillac Square, John Vachon himself was in military uniform. After his discharge, he worked briefly for Stryker again in the Standard Oil of New Jersey photographic project, became a staff photographer for *Life* and then for *Look* (where he worked for his old FSA companion Arthur Rothstein), and crowned a distinguished career as a professional photographer with the receipt of a Guggenheim Fellowship in 1973–74, shortly before his death in New York in 1975.

Sources: Carl Fleischhauer and Beverly Brannan, eds., *Documenting America, 1935–1943* (Berkeley: University of California Press in association with the Library of Congress, 1988); biographical entry by Stu Cohen in Martin Marix Evans, ed., *Contemporary Photographers*, 3d ed. (New York, 1995), 1139–40; Hank O'Neal, *A Vision Shared: A Classic Portrait of America and Its People, 1935–1943* (New York: St. Martin's Press, 1976); Archives of American Art, Smithsonian Institution, oral history interview with John Vachon; correspondence, Roy Stryker Papers, Photographic Archives, University of Louisville, microfilm edition. Quote is from Arthur Rothstein to Roy Stryker, January 1937, Roy Stryker Papers.

Arthur Rothstein (1915–85)

Arthur Rothstein enjoyed the longest association with Roy Stryker of any of the FSA/OWI photographers, and in some ways was responsible for teaching his mentor much of what Stryker came to understand about photography's possibilities and limits. A New Yorker by birth, a graduate of Stuyvesant High School, Rothstein was a student at Columbia University when he first met Roy Stryker. He worked there with Tugwell and Stryker to collect and copy photographic materials for their planned but never realized monumental pictorial study of American agriculture. For Rothstein, who was planning to become a doctor, photography had been an engrossing hobby since his boyhood, and the job for Tugwell and Stryker was merely a source of income during his lean student years. When Tugwell went to Washington to head the Resettlement Administration and called on Stryker to join him, however, Stryker in turn called on someone he knew was competent both as a lab technician and as a photographic copyist to set up the photographic laboratory for the "Historical Section."

Almost immediately Rothstein became one of the key photographers for the project, and worked in that capacity for Stryker for the next five years. A city boy who had never been far from his native New York, he was fascinated by the far west, and during his first year on the road achieved lasting fame for two images: the first that of an Oklahoma dust bowl farmer and his two sons struggling homeward against the wind of a dust storm; the other the bleached skull of a steer casting its shadow on the cracked groundscape of a drought-stricken prairie. In 1940 he left the FSA to work as a photographer for *Look* magazine. He returned briefly to work under Stryker in the Office of War Information in 1942, was drafted into the army, and served in India, Burma, and China for the U.S. Army Signal Corps, from which he returned to become *Look*'s director of photography from 1946 until its demise in 1971. He then became director of photography and later associate editor of *Parade* magazine.

Although he was the first photographer Roy Stryker hired in 1935, and became, along with Russell Lee, one of the most prolific contributors to the file, Arthur Rothstein made only one brief trip to Michigan, on an Office of War Information special assignment to portray the contributions of civilian war workers to the war effort in the industrial heartland of America. Sent to Pontiac, Michigan, where an immense Ford plant turned out vehicles for the war effort, Rothstein characteristically turned to the personal to portray a larger concept. His entire output in Michigan centered around the humble daily domestic routine and the ordinary commuting and working life of Karl Westerberg, a Swedish immigrant foreman at the plant. The few images chosen for this book from among the dozens Rothstein created have a gentle charm that illustrates the effectiveness of a photographic technique that became a staple of photojournalism—that of "the unobtrusive camera," a technique that Rothstein claimed he had originated.

Sources: biographical essay by Robert J. Doherty in Martin Marix Evans, ed., *Contemporary Photographers*, 3d ed. (New York, 1995), 972–73; O'Neal, *A Vision Shared: A Classic Portrait of America and Its People, 1935–1943* (New York: St. Martin's Press, 1976), 20–21; Archives of American Art, Smithsonian Institution, oral history interview with Arthur Rothstein; correspondence, Roy Stryker Papers, University of Louisville, microfilm edition.

BIBLIOGRAPHY

Books on Michigan

Catton, Bruce. *Michigan, A Bicentennial History*. Nashville and New York: W.W. Norton & Company, Inc. for the American Association for State and Local History, 1976.

Darden, Joe T., Richard Child Hill, June Thomas, and Richard Thomas. *Detroit: Race and Uneven Development*. Philadelphia, Penn.: Temple University Press, 1987.

Hathaway, Richard J., ed. Michigan, *Visions of our Past*. East Lansing: Michigan State University Press, 1989.

Hyde, Charles K. *Detroit: An Industrial History Guide*. Detroit: Published jointly by the Society for Industrial Archeology and the Detroit Historical Society, 1980.

Levine, David Allan. *Internal Combustion: The Races in Detroit 1915–1926*. Contributions in Afro-American and African Studies, number 24. Westport, Conn.: Greenwood Press, 1976.

Lichtenstein, Nelson. *The Most Dangerous Man in Detroit: Walter Reuther and the Fate of American Labor*. New York: Basic Books, 1995.

Meier, August, and Elliott Rudwich. *Black Detroit and the Rise of the UAW*. New York: Oxford University Press, 1979.

Sommers, Lawrence M., with Joe T. Darden, Jay R. Harman, and Laurie K. Sommers. *Michigan, A Geography*. In the series Geographies of the United States. Boulder, Colo. and London: Westview Press, 1984.

Primary Sources and Books on Documentary Photography, the FSA/OWI, Roy Stryker, and the Photographers

Anderson, James C. *Roy Stryker: The Humane Propagandist*. Louisville, Ky.: University of Louisville Photographic Archives, 1977.

Archives of American Art, Smithsonian Institution, Interviews with Jack Delano, Dorothea Lange, Russell and Jean Lee, Carl Mydans, Gordon Parks, Edwin and Louise Rosskam, Arthur Rothstein, Roy Stryker, John Vachon, Paul Vanderbilt, and Marion Post Wolcott, Microfilm Reel 3697.

Archives of American Art, Smithsonian Institution, Interviews with Charlotte Aiken, Harry Callahan, and Todd Webb, Oral History Typescripts.

Baldwin, Sidney. *Poverty and Politics: The Rise and Decline of the Farm Security Administration*. Chapel Hill: University of North Carolina Press, 1965.

Carter, John Franklin. *The Rectory Family*. New York: Coward-McCann, 1937.

Curtis, James. *Mind's Eye, Mind's Truth: FSA Photography Reconsidered*. Philadelphia, Penn.: Temple University Press, 1989.

Dick, Sheldon, and Edith Mackie. *Mexican Journey: An Intimate Guide to Mexico*. New York: Dodge Publishing Company, 1936.

Dixon, Penelope. *Photographers of the Farm Security Administration: An Annotated Bibliography, 1930–1980*. New York: Garland Publishing, 1983.

Doty, Robert, ed. *Photography in America*. New York: Whitney Museum of Art, 1974.

Evans, Martin Marix, ed. *Contemporary Photographers*. 3rd ed. New York: St. James Press, 1995.

Farm Security Administration–Office of War Information Collection. Photographs. Prints and Photographs Division, Library of Congress, Washington, D.C.

Farm Security Administration–Office of War Information Collection (P&P no. 3). Microfilm edition of lots from the FSA-OWI Collection. Photoduplication Service, Library of Congress, Washington, D.C.

Fleischhauer, Carl, and Beverly Brannan, eds. *Documenting America, 1935–1943*. Berkeley: University of California Press in association with the Library of Congress, 1988.

Guimond, James. *American Photography and the American Dream*. In Cultural Studies of the United States, edited by Alan Trachtenberg. Chapel Hill: University of North Carolina Press, 1991.

Hurley, F. Jack. *Portrait of a Decade*. Baton Rouge: Louisiana State University Press, 1972.

———. *Russell Lee, Photographer*. Dobbs Ferry, N.Y.: Morgan and Morgan, 1978.

O'Neal, Hank. *A Vision Shared: A Classic Portrait of America and Its People, 1935–1943*. New York: St. Martin's Press, 1976.

Rothstein, Arthur. *Documentary Photography*. Boston and London: Focal Press, 1986.

Stryker, Roy. Papers. Photographic Archives, University of Louisville, Louisville, Ky. Microfilm edition. Cambridge: Chadwyck-Healey Ltd., 1978–81.

Trachtenberg, Alan. *Reading American Photographs: Images as History, Mathew Brady to Walker Evans*. New York: Hill and Wang, 1989.

Winkler, Alan M. *The Politics of Propaganda: The Office of War Information, 1942–1945*. New Haven, Conn.: Yale University Press, 1978.

Wood, Nancy, and Roy Stryker. *In This Proud Land: America 1935–1943 as Seen in the FSA Photographs*. Greenwich, Conn.: New York Graphic Society, 1973.

TITLES IN THE
GREAT LAKES BOOKS SERIES

Freshwater Fury: Yarns and Reminiscences of the Greatest Storm in Inland Navigation, by Frank Barcus, 1986 (reprint)

Call It North Country: The Story of Upper Michigan, by John Bartlow Martin, 1986 (reprint)

The Land of the Crooked Tree, by U. P. Hedrick, 1986 (reprint)

Michigan Place Names, by Walter Romig, 1986 (reprint)

Luke Karamazov, by Conrad Hilberry, 1987

The Late, Great Lakes: An Environmental History, by William Ashworth, 1987 (reprint)

Great Pages of Michigan History from the Detroit Free Press, 1987

Waiting for the Morning Train: An American Boyhood, by Bruce Catton, 1987 (reprint)

Michigan Voices: Our State's History in the Words of the People Who Lived It, compiled and edited by Joe Grimm, 1987

Danny and the Boys, Being Some Legends of Hungry Hollow, by Robert Traver, 1987 (reprint)

Hanging On, or How to Get through a Depression and Enjoy Life, by Edmund G. Love, 1987 (reprint)

The Situation in Flushing, by Edmund G. Love, 1987 (reprint)

A Small Bequest, by Edmund G. Love, 1987 (reprint)

The Saginaw Paul Bunyan, by James Stevens, 1987 (reprint)

The Ambassador Bridge: A Monument to Progress, by Philip P. Mason, 1988

Let the Drum Beat: A History of the Detroit Light Guard, by Stanley D. Solvick, 1988

An Afternoon in Waterloo Park, by Gerald Dumas, 1988 (reprint)

Contemporary Michigan Poetry: Poems from the Third Coast, edited by Michael Delp, Conrad Hilberry and Herbert Scott, 1988

Over the Graves of Horses, by Michael Delp, 1988

Wolf in Sheep's Clothing: The Search for a Child Killer, by Tommy McIntyre, 1988

Copper-Toed Boots, by Marguerite de Angeli, 1989 (reprint)

Detroit Images: Photographs of the Renaissance City, edited by John J. Bukowczyk and Douglas Aikenhead, with Peter Slavcheff, 1989

Hangdog Reef: Poems Sailing the Great Lakes, by Stephen Tudor, 1989

Detroit: City of Race and Class Violence, revised edition, by B. J. Widick, 1989

Deep Woods Frontier: A History of Logging in Northern Michigan, by Theodore J. Karamanski, 1989

Orvie, The Dictator of Dearborn, by David L. Good, 1989

Seasons of Grace: A History of the Catholic Archdiocese of Detroit, by Leslie Woodcock Tentler, 1990

The Pottery of John Foster: Form and Meaning, by Gordon and Elizabeth Orear, 1990

The Diary of Bishop Frederic Baraga: First Bishop of Marquette, Michigan, edited by Regis M. Walling and Rev. N. Daniel Rupp, 1990

Walnut Pickles and Watermelon Cake: A Century of Michigan Cooking, by Larry B. Massie and Priscilla Massie, 1990

The Making of Michigan, 1820–1860: A Pioneer Anthology, edited by Justin L. Kesten-baum, 1990

America's Favorite Homes: A Guide to Popular Early Twentieth-Century Homes, by Robert Schweitzer and Michael W. R. Davis, 1990

Beyond the Model T: The Other Ventures of Henry Ford, by Ford R. Bryan, 1990

Life after the Line, by Josie Kearns, 1990

Michigan Lumbertowns: Lumbermen and Laborers in Saginaw, Bay City, and Muskegon, 1870–1905, by Jeremy W. Kilar, 1990

Detroit Kids Catalog: The Hometown Tourist, by Ellyce Field, 1990

Waiting for the News, by Leo Litwak, 1990 (reprint)

Detroit Perspectives, edited by Wilma Wood Henrickson, 1991

Life on the Great Lakes: A Wheelsman's Story, by Fred W. Dutton, edited by William Donohue Ellis, 1991

Copper Country Journal: The Diary of Schoolmaster Henry Hobart, 1863–1864, by Henry Hobart, edited by Philip P. Mason, 1991

John Jacob Astor: Business and Finance in the Early Republic, by John Denis Haeger, 1991

Survival and Regeneration: Detroit's American Indian Community, by Edmund J. Danziger, Jr., 1991

Steamboats and Sailors of the Great Lakes, by Mark L. Thompson, 1991

Cobb Would Have Caught It: The Golden Age of Baseball in Detroit, by Richard Bak, 1991

Michigan in Literature, by Clarence Andrews, 1992

Under the Influence of Water: Poems, Essays, and Stories, by Michael Delp, 1992

The Country Kitchen, by Della T. Lutes, 1992 (reprint)

The Making of a Mining District: Keweenaw Native Copper 1500–1870, by David J. Krause, 1992

Kids Catalog of Michigan Adventures, by Ellyce Field, 1993

Henry's Lieutenants, by Ford R. Bryan, 1993

Historic Highway Bridges of Michigan, by Charles K. Hyde, 1993

Lake Erie and Lake St. Clair Handbook, by Stanley J. Bolsenga and Charles E. Herndendorf, 1993

Queen of the Lakes, by Mark Thompson, 1994

Iron Fleet: The Great Lakes in World War II, by George J. Joachim, 1994

Turkey Stearnes and the Detroit Stars: The Negro Leagues in Detroit, 1919–1933, by Richard Bak, 1994

Pontiac and the Indian Uprising, by Howard H. Peckham, 1994 (reprint)

Charting the Inland Seas: A History of the U.S. Lake Survey, by Arthur M. Woodford, 1994 (reprint)

Ojibwa Narratives of Charles and Charlotte Kawbawgam and Jacques LePique, 1893–1895. Recorded with Notes by Homer H. Kidder, edited by Arthur P. Bourgeois, 1994, co-published with the Marquette County Historical Society

Strangers and Sojourners: A History of Michigan's Keweenaw Peninsula, by Arthur W. Thurner, 1994

Win Some, Lose Some: G. Mennen Williams and the New Democrats, by Helen Washburn Berthelot, 1995

Sarkis, by Gordon and Elizabeth Orear, 1995

The Northern Lights: Lighthouses of the Upper Great Lakes, by Charles K. Hyde, 1995 (reprint)

Kids Catalog of Michigan Adventures, second edition, by Ellyce Field, 1995

Rumrunning and the Roaring Twenties: Prohibition on the Michigan-Ontario Waterway, by Philip P. Mason, 1995

In the Wilderness with the Red Indians, by E. R. Baierlein, translated by Anita Z. Boldt, edited by Harold W. Moll, 1996

Elmwood Endures: History of a Detroit Cemetery, by Michael Franck, 1996

Master of Precision: Henry M. Leland, by Mrs. Wilfred C. Leland with Minnie Dubbs Millbrook, 1996 (reprint)

Haul-Out: New and Selected Poems, by Stephen Tudor, 1996

Kids Catalog of Michigan Adventures, third edition, by Ellyce Field, 1997

Beyond the Model T: The Other Ventures of Henry Ford, revised edition, by Ford R. Bryan, 1997

Young Henry Ford: A Picture History of the First Forty Years, by Sidney Olson, 1997 (reprint)

The Coast of Nowhere: Meditations on Rivers, Lakes and Streams, by Michael Delp, 1997

From Saginaw Valley to Tin Pan Alley: Saginaw's Contribution to American Popular Music, 1890–1955, by R. Grant Smith, 1998

The Long Winter Ends, by Newton G. Thomas, 1998 (reprint)

Bridging the River of Hatred: The Pioneering Efforts of Detroit Police Commissioner George Edwards, by Mary M. Stolberg, 1998

Toast of the Town: The Life and Times of Sunnie Wilson, by Sunnie Wilson with John Cohassey, 1998

These Men Have Seen Hard Service: The First Michigan Sharpshooters in the Civil War, by Raymond J. Herek, 1998

A Place for Summer: One Hundred Years at Michigan and Trumbull, by Richard Bak, 1998

Early Midwestern Travel Narratives: An Annotated Bibliography, 1634–1850, by Robert R. Hubach, 1998 (reprint)

All-American Anarchist: Joseph A. Labadie and the Labor Movement, by Carlotta R. Anderson, 1998

Michigan in the Novel, 1816–1996: An Annotated Bibliography, by Robert Beasecker, 1998

"Time by Moments Steals Away": The 1848 Journal of Ruth Douglass, by Robert L. Root, Jr., 1998

The Detroit Tigers: A Pictorial Celebration of the Greatest Players and Moments in Tigers' History, updated edition, by William M. Anderson, 1999

Father Abraham's Children: Michigan Episodes in the Civil War, by Frank B. Woodford, 1999 (reprint)

Letter from Washington, 1863–1865, by Lois Bryan Adams, edited and with an introduction by Evelyn Leasher, 1999

Wonderful Power: The Story of Ancient Copper Working in the Lake Superior Basin, by Susan R. Martin, 1999

A Sailor's Logbook: A Season aboard Great Lakes Freighters, by Mark L. Thompson, 1999

Huron: The Seasons of a Great Lake, by Napier Shelton, 1999

Tin Stackers: The History of the Pittsburgh Steamship Company, by Al Miller, 1999

Art in Detroit Public Places, revised edition, text by Dennis Nawrocki, photographs by David Clements, 1999

Brewed in Detroit: Breweries and Beers Since 1830, by Peter H. Blum, 1999

Detroit Kids Catalog: A Family Guide for the 21st Century, by Ellyce Field, 2000

"Expanding the Frontiers of Civil Rights": Michigan, 1948–1968, by Sidney Fine, 2000

Graveyard of the Lakes, by Mark L. Thompson, 2000

Enterprising Images: The Goodridge Brothers, African American Photographers, 1847–1922, by John Vincent Jezierski, 2000

New Poems from the Third Coast: Contemporary Michigan Poetry, edited by Michael Delp, Conrad Hilberry, and Josie Kearns, 2000

Arab Detroit: From Margin to Mainstream, edited by Nabeel Abraham and Andrew Shryock, 2000

The Sandstone Architecture of the Lake Superior Region, by Kathryn Bishop Eckert, 2000

Looking Beyond Race: The Life of Otis Milton Smith, by Otis Milton Smith and Mary M. Stolberg, 2000

Mail by the Pail, by Colin Bergel, illustrated by Mark Koenig, 2000

Great Lakes Journey: A New Look at America's Freshwater Coast, by William Ashworth, 2000

A Life in the Balance: The Memoirs of Stanley J. Winkelman, by Stanley J. Winkelman, 2000

Schooner Passage: Sailing Ships and the Lake Michigan Frontier, by Theodore J. Karamanski, 2000

The Outdoor Museum: The Magic of Michigan's Marshall M. Fredericks, by Marcy Heller Fisher, illustrated by Christine Collins Woomer, 2001

Detroit in Its World Setting: A Three Hundred Year Chronology, 1701–2001, edited by David Lee Poremba, 2001

Frontier Metropolis: Picturing Early Detroit, 1701–1838, by Brian Leigh Dunnigan, 2001

Michigan Remembered: Photographs from the Farm Security Administration and the Office of War Information, 1936–1943, edited by Constance B. Schulz, with Introductory Essays by Constance B. Schulz and William H. Mulligan, Jr., 2001